World Health Organization
Regional Office for Europe
Copenhagen

Evaluation and monitoring of action on alcohol

Targets, indicators and monitoring and reporting systems for action on alcohol

by

Peter Anderson
Alcohol, Drugs and Tobacco Unit
WHO Regional Office for Europe

and

Juhani Lehto
National Research and Development Centre
for Welfare and Health, Helsinki, Finland

WHO Regional Publications, European Series, No. 59

Text editing by Mary Stewart Burgher

WHO Library Cataloguing in Publication Data

Anderson, Peter

Evaluation and monitoring of action on alcohol : targets, indicators and monitoring and reporting systems for action on alcohol / by Peter Anderson and Juhani Lehto

(WHO regional publications. European series ; No. 59)

1.Alcoholism - prevention and control 2.Health policy 3.Health plan implementation 4.Evaluation studies 5.Europe I.Lehto, Juhani II.Title III.Series

ISBN 92 890 1323 0 (LC Classification: HV 5082)
ISSN 0378–2255

The designations employed and the presentation of the material in this publication do not imply the expression of any opinion whatsoever on the part of the Secretariat of the World Health Organization concerning the legal status of any country, territory, city or area or of its authorities, or concerning the delimitation of its frontiers or boundaries. The names of countries or areas used in this publication are those that obtained at the time the original language edition of the book was prepared.

The mention of specific companies or of certain manufacturers' products does not imply that they are endorsed or recommended by the World Health Organization in preference to others of a similar nature that are not mentioned. Errors and omissions excepted, the names of proprietary products are distinguished by initial capital letters.

The views expressed in this publication are those of the authors and do not necessarily represent the decisions or the stated policy of the World Health Organization.

PRINTED IN FINLAND

Contents

Introduction

The health policy for the WHO European Region, as expressed in 38 targets, lists the improvements in health that are needed to secure health for all Europeans by the year 2000 *(1)*. Target 17 addresses alcohol consumption.

Alcohol is of particular concern for the Region because of the high level of its production, global trade and consumption and the extent of associated problems *(2)*. The Region faces a complex future, with a trend towards political liberalization and the attendant difficulties of evaluating and predicting changes in the central and eastern countries. In this context, alcohol should be viewed as a special commodity, because of its dependence-producing properties and the severity of the problems associated with its use. Most of these problems, if not all, can be prevented.

The European Alcohol Action Plan was prepared to support the attainment of target 17 through work for significant reductions in the harmful consumption of alcohol in all Member States *(3)*. The Action Plan proposes a comprehensive public health policy on alcohol at the European, national and local levels. Such policies would combine control measures with action by the community, the health services and other sectors, including social welfare, education and criminal justice. The Plan advocates both measures to reduce overall levels of alcohol consumption (a population-based approach) and specific measures aimed at risk behaviour (a high-risk approach). In September 1992, the WHO Regional Committee for Europe strongly endorsed the Action Plan as a positive set of guidelines for Member States to follow.

One of the ideas underpinning the targets for health for all is that effective public health policy needs clear objectives and targets, and that the attainment of or progress towards the targets should be monitored and evaluated. The monitoring and evaluation should give feedback to political decision-makers, administrators and everyone who is responsible for the implementation of the policy. These people need the information to develop, update or restructure the policy and its components, as well as to assess the ways in which it is implemented.

One of the first priorities for work under the European Alcohol Action Plan is thus to clarify objectives, set targets, agree on indicators and create monitoring and evaluation systems at the international, national and local levels. This publication, the first in a series of nine, is based on the experiences of WHO and many countries in developing their knowledge bases on alcohol consumption, related problems and social responses. A WHO working group discussed the first draft in Copenhagen in September 1992.

This publication presents proposals for "subtargets" of target 17, and for indicators and data sources for use in monitoring and evaluation. The information that is or may be available varies considerably between countries, so monitoring and evaluation systems cannot be identical. Nevertheless, the Region as a whole and its Member States would benefit if as many countries as possible used at least a minimum number of indicators that have been proved to be the most easily available and best to reflect the overall attainment of the targets. Such indicators are also required for international comparison and evaluation.

This publication contains six chapters. The first discusses the 38 targets of the health policy for Europe, which the Member States of the WHO European Region have adopted. The second chapter discusses potential targets and indicators for action on alcohol. The third, fourth and fifth suggest alcohol action targets and indicators for the European, national and local levels, respectively. The last chapter summarizes the opportunities for and the conditions and benefits of setting clear targets, using indicators to monitor their attainment and evaluating action on alcohol.

1

Targets for Health for All

The health policy for Europe and its 38 targets specify the improvements in health that are needed to secure health for all in the Region *(1)*. The targets (Annex 1) call for:

- particular improvements in health status between levels in 1980 and those in the year 2000 (targets 1–12);
- the changes in lifestyles (targets 13–17), the improvements in the environment (targets 18–25) and the developments in prevention, treatment, care and rehabilitation services (targets 26–31) that will enable the attainment of these improvements; and
- the formulation and sustained implementation of policy through political, managerial and institutional support and coordination (targets 32–38).

The health outcomes that the health for all movement is striving to achieve have four dimensions:

1. ensuring equity in health, by reducing disparities in health status between countries and between groups within countries;
2. adding life to years by helping people to achieve and use their full physical, mental and social potential;
3. adding health to life by reducing disease and disability; and
4. adding years to life by increasing life expectancy.

TARGET 17

Target 17 is one of the five lifestyles targets, and states the objective of the European Alcohol Action Plan. It is also the basis for the Action Plan for a Tobacco-free Europe and for action to reduce the demand for psychoactive drugs (*1*):

> By the year 2000, the health-damaging consumption of dependence-producing substances such as alcohol, tobacco and psychoactive drugs should have been significantly reduced in all Member States.
>
> This target can be achieved if well balanced policies and programmes in regard to the consumption and production of these substances are implemented at all levels and in different sectors to:
>
> - increase the number of nonsmokers to at least 80% of the population and protect nonsmokers from involuntary exposure to tobacco smoke;
> - reduce alcohol consumption by 25%, with particular attention to reducing harmful use;
> - obtain a sustained and continuing reduction in the abuse of psychoactive drugs, including inappropriate use of prescribed drugs.

The baseline for the 25% reduction is the level of alcohol consumption in 1980.

In addition to attaining target 17, the Action Plan contributes to the attainment of the 12 targets on health status. A decrease in alcohol consumption would help to reduce many chronic diseases, such as cardiovascular diseases and cancer, as well as accidents and mental disorders. It would also contribute to the health of women and children. Excessive alcohol consumption is a risk factor for many communicable diseases, including HIV infection. Finally, alcohol policy may contribute to the achievement of the targets on equity in health and quality of life.

At the same time, the implementation of the Action Plan is linked with the attainment of the targets on promoting health, improving the environment and developing health services and health policies. For instance, the Action Plan advocates intersectoral public health policy and action in cities, schools and workplaces. It is linked with health promotion at work and the development of primary health care. It also needs support from health policy development in general (targets 32–38).

THE NATURE OF TARGETS

A strategic approach to health care planning requires the identification of specific goals (health outcomes) for improvement in the population's health. These need to be interpreted in terms of the quality of life as well as the quantity (health gains). The description of the current position and the charting of progress towards such goals, however, often require the identification of intermediate objectives, not only for health but also for the important determinants of health and the processes that lead to changes in these factors. These may be necessary because improvements in health status are delayed or because they bear a complicated relationship to multiple causal factors, and therefore interventions are better aimed at individual determinants.

If objectives are to be useful in guiding the design of policies and programmes, they should be accompanied by measurable indicators describing levels of health, the determinants of health concerned and levels of relevant services and protection. Further, the indicators need to be sensitive to the size of the changes that are anticipated. Once indicators have been identified, targets can be set that will suggest the pace at which progress towards the objectives could reasonably be expected.

As any strategy tends to have much less impact if its implementation cannot be subsequently evaluated, appropriate information is a prerequisite for effective strategic planning.

SETTING TARGETS

Problems

The process of setting targets can involve several problems, both theoretical and practical *(4–6)*. The first is how to reduce health to quantifiable indicators and targets. Once a numerical target is defined, the next problem is to judge what improvement one might expect, want or hope for by the year 2000. One can either extrapolate trends, with greater or lesser mathematical sophistication, or take some arbitrary normative stance. In general, one should prefer informed judgement to elaborate modelling, and round targets off to avoid any spurious impression of precision. The practical problems are mostly those of data availability. For example, some pertinent data are not collected at all.

Numerical targets can be used to highlight important areas of a strategy and are useful in the process of converting policy into programmes. They also provide a tangible means of monitoring progress and can act as a stimulus for the collection of good data. The disadvantages of numerical targets are, however, that:

- they can lead to a spurious priority being given to what is measurable;
- if taken in isolation, they represent a simplistic description of policy; and
- unless the desired levels are carefully chosen, they can appear unrealistic and be easily dismissed as unattainable.

Thus, there is no need to have only numerical targets. It is much easier to develop them for health outcomes than for the processes and policies leading to these outcomes. Nevertheless, using numerical targets brings many benefits, particularly in the monitoring and evaluation of attainment. By considering, at the developmental stage, the problems of numerical targets and certain principles for avoiding these problems, one can improve the usefulness of targets.

Special Populations

Attention should focus on groups at high risk, with the aim of eliminating health disparities between them and the population as a whole. Special targets should be set when a group has shown a high risk of disease. This risk may be defined in terms of either higher rates than those for the overall population or different trends.

Targets for special populations should be realistic. They may need to be set for countries or regions within them, ethnic minority groups and certain age, sex and occupational groups.

Guiding Principles

The guiding principles for the development of targets include credibility, public comprehension, responsibility, balance, measurability, continuity and freedom from data constraints. This means that targets should:

- reflect available scientific evidence on potential health benefits, be realistic and address the issues of greatest priority;
- be understandable and relevant to a broad audience, including the people who plan, manage, deliver, use and pay for health services;
- reflect the concerns and engage the participation of professionals, public health advocates and consumers, as well as governments and health departments;
- include both outcome and process measures, thus recommending methods for achieving changes and setting standards for evaluating progress;
- be compatible, when possible, with the goals already adopted by governments and health organizations;
- be quantified; and
- not be determined primarily by the availability of data, but use alternative and proxy data while maintaining a commitment to evaluation.

2

Potential Targets Related to Alcohol

This chapter discusses the opportunities to translate the objectives proposed in the European Alcohol Action Plan into targets. Most of the discussion focuses on the national level, but the conclusions can also be used to define targets at the international and local levels. The potential targets are discussed under the headings of objectives for alcohol use, health status, social and economic factors and policy.

ALCOHOL USE

Recorded Alcohol Consumption

Many countries have good records on national alcohol consumption because of tax and excise on alcoholic beverages. Routinely collected national data are also available for production, trade and consumption. Rather reliable data on recorded alcohol consumption can be obtained from three alternative sources:

- statistics on taxation, especially in countries that have particular excise taxes for each type of alcoholic beverage (when the amount consumed in a country may be estimated to equal the amount for which taxes are paid);
- the sales statistics collected from wholesale or retail companies or by their organizations; and
- the statistics on production and trade (and stocks) of alcoholic beverages.

As to the third source, the amount consumed in a country may be estimated to equal the volume of production, plus the volume of imports, and minus the volume of exports and the increase in stocks. In most countries, the change in stocks may be assumed to be insignificant in comparison to overall consumption.

Data on consumption per head are derived from statistics produced by Member States on the volume sold or released for consumption. They do not cover duty-free purchases, purchases imported for personal use, alcohol released from stocks, or non-recorded beverages such as ciders in France. They relate only to drinks legally recorded as wines, beers or spirits and therefore underestimate consumption, particularly in some of the countries of central and eastern Europe and the former USSR *(7)*. Nevertheless, some of the figures may overestimate consumption by domestic populations, owing to consumption by tourists where their numbers are significant in relation to the domestic population.

The overall change in the consumption per head of pure alcohol must be calculated from bulk volume series by assuming average alcohol strengths. There are no consistent series estimating the approximate strengths of beers, wines or spirits consumed in different countries. Series derived from production figures do not necessarily reflect the strengths of drinks consumed in many countries.

In some countries, customs and excise data are available for long periods of time. They are readily available and provide information on beers, wines and spirits. In most countries, these data are collected from production or warehouse facilities, not at the point of sale. This results in many difficulties in obtaining accurate consumption data at the municipal or district level. In addition, sales can be used to provide information on nonalcoholic and low-alcohol beers and wines.

Unrecorded Alcohol Consumption

Routinely collected production and tax data do not cover all the consumption of alcohol *(8)*. The main reasons for documenting unrecorded consumption are the following.

The first is to secure complete statistical accuracy in figures on total alcohol consumption. Second, variations in unrecorded consumption may indicate important changes in drinking patterns. For example, an increase in the production of home-made wines or beers may point to a growth in hobbies. Third, unrecorded consumption is important for studies on the interaction between alcohol policies and public attitudes and behaviour. Fourth, illegal and home-produced alcohol may contain impurities such as methanol, which result in health risks in addition to those related to ethanol.

Data on unrecorded consumption can be collected under four headings: unrecorded or home production, unrecorded imports, unrecorded consumption by alcohol industry employees and the consumption of non-beverage alcohol. Such data can be obtained from the following sources:

- government control and crime statistics on medicines, smuggled spirits, home-distilled liquors and denatured spirits;
- sales statistics on raw materials and supplies, such as yeasts, distilling equipment and crushed barley malt for home-made beer;
- estimates by experts;
- observation; and
- surveys.

Repeated National Surveys

In a number of countries, data on alcohol use are collected routinely through national surveys conducted every one or two years. For example, some annual surveys cover many topics, which may include alcohol use. In the United Kingdom, the General Household Survey *(9)* and the Family Expenditure Survey *(10)* comprise interviews of some 10 000 households, using questions about the quantity and frequency of alcohol use and detailed diaries to record information on expenditure on alcoholic beverages.

The main problem with general surveys that record information about alcohol is that they often measure consumption in a variety of ways. This impairs comparisons between surveys, and between different time periods within the same series of surveys. Uniformity and consistency are needed. Annex 2 provides a more detailed discussion of this topic.

Detailed surveys on drinking habits are made less frequently than the general surveys in the United Kingdom. For example, the Finnish drinking habits surveys, with interviews of 2000–3600 people, have been conducted every eight years since 1968 *(11)*. They provide information on the distribution of alcohol consumption among the population, how drinking habits change, what motivates drinking or abstinence, and people's attitudes towards alcohol and the various consequences of using it.

Regular surveys of drinking habits are needed for monitoring and evaluation, if it is decided to set targets such as decreasing the proportion of heavy drinkers (people who drink over a defined amount of alcohol per day or week), drinking among certain population groups (such as young people, women or middle-aged men) or other high-risk drinking (such as that leading to intoxication).

The small numbers in each sample means that national ad hoc surveys provide little useful regional data. Local population surveys with sufficient numbers could be expensive, but would be needed to monitor local trends. Central guidance and the use of existing data would be important parts of ensuring the local implementation of any alcohol strategy.

Although drinking surveys underestimate the total amount of alcohol consumed, compared with tax data, the biases are likely to be consistent over time. Thus, the surveys allow the study of changes in drinking patterns and differences between the sexes and various age groups *(12,13)*.

International Surveys

Some ad hoc surveys have been made at the international level, in western Europe *(14,15)*. They have given some insight into the differences in drinking habits between countries (Table 1) but their many methodological problems mean that their reliability is not very high.

Table 1. Proportion of abstainers and daily drinkers among those aged over 18 years in western Europe, 1990

Country	Abstainers (%)	Daily drinkers (%)
Italy	19	43
Portugal	31	33
France	14	27
Switzerland	12	18
Spain	36	17
Luxembourg	26	17
Netherlands	16	17
Germany	9	16
Belgium	23	14
Denmark	4	14
Austria	6	12
Great Britain	14	11
Greece	25	10
Ireland	25	3
Finland	18	3
Sweden	14	1
Norway	15	1

Source: Reader's Digest Eurodata – a consumer survey of 17 European countries (15).

A WHO cross-national survey of health behaviour in school-age children *(16)* has been undertaken in a growing number of European Member States. It includes some questions on drinking habits, and is repeated every four years. It gives insight into the trends in alcohol consumption among teenagers.

Potential Targets

Potential targets on alcohol use could focus on:

- the total consumption of alcohol; and
- the frequency of high-risk drinking, including:
  - the prevalence of heavy drinking
  - the prevalence of high-risk drinking among young people

- the frequency of drinking leading to intoxication
- the frequency of high-risk drinking among certain population groups.

HEALTH STATUS

The harm done by alcohol use to physical, social and psychological health has been extensively reviewed *(17–19)*. Alcohol is not only the cause, by definition, of conditions such as alcohol dependence and alcoholic psychosis, but also the most significant risk factor for others, such as chronic liver diseases, and a more or less significant risk factor for a wide range of other diseases and causes of death *(20–22)*. The latter include cancer, cardiovascular diseases, accidents, suicide, injuries caused by violence and communicable diseases.

Different patterns of drinking are linked with different diseases. For example, liver cirrhosis is linked to regular heavy use, while accidents can result from drinking on single occasions.

The list of health damage related to alcohol use is still growing. One of the recent probable additions is cancer of the female breast. Owing to the importance of breast cancer as a cause of death for women and the lack of other effective policy options for population-based prevention, this important finding emphasizes the significant public health benefits of reducing alcohol consumption.

On the one hand, heavy alcohol consumption is associated with a large number of diseases, and reducing it would result in health gain. On the other hand, some evidence shows that low levels of alcohol consumption, compared with no consumption, reduce the risk of coronary heart disease; this topic has been reviewed extensively elsewhere *(22–24)*. Nevertheless, the evidence for an increased risk of accidents and other health problems at rather low consumption is strong enough to preclude support for a public health message to increase alcohol consumption in order to prevent coronary heart disease.

Available Data

The most important data on alcohol-related health problems include those on mortality, traffic accidents, the treatment of alcohol-related health problems, and disability pensions and sickness absenteeism.

Mortality data are ordinarily collected from death certificates written by attending physicians. Death certificates vary considerably in both the accuracy and rates of recording for cirrhosis, alcoholic psychosis and other alcohol-related conditions. Incorrect entries may be common, owing either to negligence or to diagnostic error. For example, a physician may record ischaemic heart disease as the cause of death, rather than cardiomyopathy of alcoholic origin, and conditions related to chronic alcoholism are sometimes omitted.

Data on mortality from diseases for which alcohol is only one of many risk factors are available in all Member States. Estimating the proportion of these deaths, in different countries and at different times, that can be attributed to alcohol is rather difficult. Many countries, however, have carried out studies on the role of alcohol in some of these deaths, such as those from traffic and other accidents and violence. For example, the Centers for Disease Control *(20)* has estimated the role of alcohol in various causes of death in the United States (Table 2). Such estimates probably vary between countries and over time, owing to differences in drinking habits and in the impact of other risk factors.

Data on alcohol-related traffic accidents can be obtained in many countries from statistics collected by the police or by motor insurance companies. Like mortality statistics, these data vary widely in both accuracy and the recording rates for the involvement of alcohol.

Data on morbidity from alcohol-related diseases are routinely available only indirectly, through data on the utilization of health services. In some countries, a significant part of the specialized treatment of alcohol dependence is organized under the social welfare administration, so data from this sector should be added to those from health services. Routinely collected data may include admissions to inpatient treatment for conditions such as liver cirrhosis, alcohol dependence, alcohol withdrawal syndrome and alcoholic psychosis.

Table 2. Proportion of deaths from various causes that is attributable to alcohol, United States, 1990

Cause of death	%
Cancer of the lip, oral cavity and pharynx	
Males	50
Females	40
Cancer of the oesophagus	75
Cancer of the stomach	20
Cancer of the liver	15
Cancer of the larynx	
Males	50
Females	40
Alcoholic psychosis	100
Alcohol dependency syndrome	100
Alcohol withdrawal syndrome	100
Essential hypertension	8
Alcoholic cardiomyopathy	100
Cerebrovascular disease	7
Pulmonary tuberculosis	25
Pneumonia and influenza	5
Diseases of the oesophagus, stomach and duodenum	10
Gastritis caused by alcohol	100
Alcohol fatty liver	100
Acute alcohol hepatitis	100
Alcoholic cirrhosis of the liver	100
Alcoholic liver damage, unspecified	100
Cirrhosis of the liver, without mention of alcohol	50
Acute pancreatitis	42
Chronic pancreatitis	60
Motor vehicle traffic and non-traffic accidents	42
Pedal cycle accidents	20
Water sport accidents	20
Air and space transport accidents	16
Accidental poisonings by alcohol	100
Accidental falls	35
Accidents caused by fire	45
Accidental drownings	38
Other accidents	25
Suicide and self-inflicted injury	28
Homicide and purposely inflicted injury	46
Diabetes mellitus	5
Alcoholic polyneuropathy	100
Excessive blood level of alcohol	100

Source: Centers for Disease Control *(20)*

In addition, some countries have data on the use of outpatient services and primary health care services to manage alcohol-related problems.

Treatment data never directly reflect morbidity; they are influenced by the supply of services. Thus, changes in numbers of people treated may indicate changes in morbidity, changes in treatment provision or both. This is particularly important for data on the treatment of alcohol dependence. Data on the treatment of more serious problems, such as alcoholic psychosis, more closely reflect actual changes in morbidity *(25)*.

In addition, the number of new and old disability pensions and number of days spent on sick-leave reflect morbidity from various causes. In some countries, such data are collected routinely. They may include data on alcohol-related diseases and thus give information about the active working time lost due to alcohol. Diagnostic practices change with time, however, and a client may have an interest in hiding the role of alcohol in the development of a disabling disease. As a result, these data are often rather unreliable regarding alcohol-related problems. In addition, the frequent changes in social security systems make using the data rather complicated.

In principle, the analysis of alcohol-related health problems should do more than calculate deaths and the prevalence and incidence of different diseases. An estimate of the active years of life that are lost due to different alcohol-related problems could give a better picture of the potential health gains from reduced alcohol consumption. In particular, this approach emphasizes accidents as a significant alcohol-related health problem.

Quality of Available Data

Some problems related to the quality of the data on alcohol-related mortality and morbidity have already been mentioned. They necessitate caution in making comparisons between countries or regions in a country. Very often the data are more reliable in describing trends in a geographic area than in making comparisons between areas at a given time.

Most of the available data are collected at the national level, although the WHO Regional Office for Europe collects some for its health for all database on the Region (see Chapter 3). In many countries, some data are also available at the regional, district or municipal level.

Potential Targets

Potential targets on health status, measured in mortality, morbidity or years of life lost, could focus on:

- chronic diseases, including cirrhosis of the liver;
- maternal and infant health, including fetal alcohol syndrome;
- cardiovascular diseases, including stroke and high blood pressure;
- cancer, including cancers of the upper aerodigestive tract and cancer of the female breast;
- accidents and injuries, including:
  - homicide;
  - assault injuries;
  - alcohol-related road traffic accidents;
  - unintentional injuries;
  - head injuries;
  - work-related injuries; and
- mental health problems, including:
  - suicide;
  - depression;
  - alcohol dependence, alcohol withdrawal syndrome and alcoholic psychosis.

SOCIAL AND ECONOMIC FACTORS

In addition to health damage, the social problems and economic costs related to alcohol use have been reviewed *(26)*.

The social problems include child abuse, violence and other problems in the family, poverty, disturbances of public order, decreased traffic safety and crime. They have a significant impact on public health, because they increase the risk of many problems related to physical, social and psychological health. Different patterns and contexts of drinking and different social responses to drinking may lead to different social problems. For example, rather moderate drinking in an otherwise stressful situation might lead to problems that would not otherwise occur.

Most alcohol-related social problems are multifactorial, resulting from the combined influence of alcohol and various other factors. Because the relative significance of these factors varies between countries and over time, calculating the percentage of problems attributable to alcohol is impossible. Nevertheless, many studies indicate that, other factors being equal, a decrease in alcohol consumption leads to a decrease in many social problems *(27)*.

The economic costs include the costs of alcohol-related health and social problems for individuals, families, employers, public authorities and society. They include the expense to households of buying alcoholic beverages, as well as the costs of social responses to problems, such as treatment, prevention, social welfare and criminal justice. They also include the costs of subsidies for the production of or trade in alcoholic beverages, as well as the social and environmental costs of these activities.

In addition, alcohol brings some social and economic benefits. These include the pleasures attributed to drinking, and employment in producing and serving alcoholic beverages. The revenue from tax and excise on alcohol is a significant benefit for the state treasury.

A decrease in alcohol consumption should lead to a decrease in production and trade. Otherwise, lower consumption in one country would lead to pressure for an increase at a later stage or in other countries. In particular, the big alcohol producers in western Europe may try to compensate for decreasing consumption at home by increased exports abroad, including developing countries.

Available Data on Alcohol-related Social Problems

Different sectors of public administration routinely collect data that can be used to monitor and evaluate alcohol-related social problems.

In many countries, social welfare and social service authorities collect data on, for example:

- problems behind known cases of child abuse or child neglect;
- problems behind the need for last-resort social allowances;
- problems of the users of services for family problems; and
- the treatment of alcohol problems in specialized social services.

In most countries, the police collect data on, for example:

- arrests for drunkenness;
- arrests for disturbances of public order;
- alerts and/or arrests for family violence;
- crime reported to and investigated by the police; and
- drink-drivers apprehended through accidents or random breath testing.

In many countries, other parts of the criminal justice system may collect data on such issues as:

- the frequency of alcohol-related problems among prisoners; and
- treatment of alcohol problems as a part of or as an alternative to a prison sentence.

Such data are not usually direct indicators of alcohol-related problems. They refer to activities that respond to problems that are very often or always related to alcohol use. Changes in the number of these activities may reflect changes in the scale of the problems or in the activities of the social welfare or criminal justice authorities. For example, an increase in random breath testing by the police may decrease drink-driving, but increase the number of drink-drivers caught.

Used with consideration of these problems and sufficient caution, these data would add significantly to the monitoring and evaluation of alcohol-related problems and social responses. The problems with using social data are much the same as those of using treatment data as indicators of morbidity.

Potential Targets

Potential targets on social wellbeing or social problems could focus on:

- social welfare, including the neglect of children and the need for last-resort social allowances;
- public order, including arrests for drunkenness and disturbing public order, and police alerts for family violence;
- traffic safety, including drink-drivers caught by the police; and
- crime, including crimes committed under the influence of alcohol and the frequency of alcohol problems among prisoners.

Available Data on Alcohol-related Economic Costs

The economic costs due to alcohol, and sometimes the economic benefits, are an important aspect of the monitoring and evaluation of alcohol policy.

Most of the data on costs have to be calculated on the basis of data on alcohol-related problems and responses to them. Such data thus provide an alternative picture of alcohol problems.

The economic costs of alcohol use reflect approximately the level of alcohol-related health and social problems in a country, although the costs of social responses may also reflect the priority given to them (Table 3). Because the frequency of many alcohol-related problems is directly related to the overall consumption of alcohol, the economic costs are also expected to reflect total consumption.

The relationship between the total consumption of alcohol and economic benefits is more complex. For example, raising the taxes on alcohol may both increase state revenue and decrease alcohol consumption. It would be wrong to assume that such a decrease in consumption would always decrease employment; it would allow an increase in consumption in other sectors, such as non-alcoholic drinks and leisure-time services. Thus, an increase in employment in the production of other commodities and services would probably compensate for a decrease in employment in alcohol production and trade.

Estimates of costs and benefits are a useful part of the information for the evaluation of alcohol policies. In particular, they emphasize the large economic benefits that rather small investments in preventing problems and promoting health can achieve. Nevertheless, the changes in costs do not always reflect changes in the number and seriousness of the problems, and many cost calculations are rough second- or third-order estimates (based on the estimates of alcohol-related health and social problems and estimates of the costs of these problems). Creating adequate indicators of the overall costs of alcohol is therefore a difficult task.

Available Data on Alcohol Production and Trade

Many countries have reliable data on the production and trade of alcoholic beverages, and intergovernmental organizations, such as the Food and Agriculture Organization of the United Nations (FAO), the Organisation for Economic Co-operation and Development (OECD) and the European Union (EU), collect some data. Such information is particularly useful for evaluating the economic and political strength of the alcohol industry, emphasizing the need for international co-operation and anticipating future pressures on alcohol policy. Because the alcohol industry mainly affects public health through consumption, in addition to its effects on environmental and occupational health, no specific targets and indicators are suggested at the European level.

POLICY OBJECTIVES

The European Alcohol Action Plan proposes a comprehensive public health policy on alcohol that combines action at different levels, from different sectors of society and using a range of policy measures. The

Table 3. Estimates of costs of alcohol-related social problems and of some social responses in the United Kingdom

Problem or response	Cost (£ million)
Industry	
Sickness absence	964.37
Housework services	64.78
Unemployment	222.23
Premature death	870.76
Material damage	
Material damage in alcohol-related traffic accidents	138.62
Criminal activities	
Police involvement in traffic offences:	
excluding road traffic accidents	6.53
including judiciary and insurance administration	19.36
Alcohol-related court cases	24.18
National Health Service	
Psychiatric hospitals: inpatient costs for treatment of alcoholic psychosis, alcohol dependence syndrome, non-dependent use of alcohol	26.51
Non-psychiatric hospitals: inpatient costs for treatment of alcohol dependence syndrome, alcoholic cirrhosis and liver disease	10.64
Other alcohol-related inpatient costs	109.41
General practice	2.79
Other responses	
Expenditure on national health education programmes	0.44
Research	0.80
Total	
Excluding unemployment and premature death	1368.43
Including unemployment and premature death	2461.42

Source: Godfrey & Hardman *(26)*.

Plan demonstrates this comprehensive approach by calling for action in nine strategic areas to prevent and manage the harm done by alcohol use. It calls for action *(3)*:

1. to strengthen policies for prevention in Member States;
2. to build consensus among intergovernmental organizations on joint action for prevention;
3. to strengthen practices in the alcohol and hospitality industries that support prevention;
4. to create and sustain action in certain settings that strengthens people's motivation and capacity to avoid harmful drinking;
5. to support community action for prevention and management;
6. to strengthen public support for safer alcohol drinking practices through educational programmes;
7. to strengthen the contribution of health care systems, and particularly primary health care, to prevention and management;
8. to strengthen the contribution of the social welfare system to prevention; and
9. to strengthen the contribution of the criminal justice system to prevention.

Most of the objectives for health status, social wellbeing and economic cost are clearly quantitative. Their aim is to decrease the number of alcohol-related deaths, other alcohol-related problems, and the active years lost or amount of money spent. The policy objectives have a more qualitative nature, but contain some quantitative aspects. For example, an objective could be that an increased proportion of schools implement certain health education programmes.

National and Subnational Alcohol Policy

Well balanced alcohol policies have been shown to have clear preventive value *(22,28)*. Effective measures to reduce alcohol-related problems include the control of alcohol availability through the regulation of production and trade, the setting of a minimum legal drinking age, restrictions on alcohol advertising, and increases in prices and taxes. The making of comparisons between countries or regions requires information on the content of legislation and the success of its enforcement, and on the price and tax level of alcoholic beverages, preferably compared with the prices of and taxes on other consumer goods.

Potential Targets

Potential targets on alcohol policy could focus on:

- the extent and effectiveness of the control of alcohol production, exports, imports, and wholesale and retail sales;
- controls on advertising;
- a minimum drinking age and other restrictions on drinking alcoholic beverages;
- an increase in the real prices of alcoholic beverages;
- a legal limit of blood alcohol concentration in drivers of motor vehicles; and
- the extent of random testing of drivers of motor vehicles.

Policies of Intergovernmental Organizations

The policies of intergovernmental organizations such as EU can have a significant impact on alcohol consumption and the harm done by alcohol use *(29,30)*. For example, EU taxation policies may lead to reductions in the price of alcohol in some countries (such as Denmark, Ireland, the United Kingdom and countries bordering the EU) and higher prices in others (such as Portugal and Spain). EU subsidies to the producers of wine and other alcoholic drinks have a significant impact on alcohol supply. The EU directive on the content of alcohol advertising on television and the preparation of other international control policies could have an impact at the national and subnational levels *(31)*.

Potential Targets

Potential targets for intergovernmental organizations could focus on:

- the extent of subsidies for alcohol production and trade;
- the impact of fiscal measures on alcohol prices;

- the extent of international control policies; and
- the extent of support for other public health policies on alcohol.

Preventive Practices of the Alcohol and Hospitality Industries

The alcohol and hospitality industries could have an interest in certain areas of prevention. These include the discouragement of drinking and driving, education on the hazards of drinking during pregnancy and the development of server training programmes. The latter could enable alcohol servers to do more to prevent excessive drinking, drinking and driving, and drinking by people under the minimum legal age. In many countries, the threat of tight legislative restriction on advertising has led the alcohol industry to adopt self-regulatory codes of marketing *(32,33)*.

Potential Targets

Potential targets for the alcohol and hospitality industries could focus on:

- the extent of their influence on decision-making on alcohol policy;
- the quality and extent of their prevention programmes; and
- the quality of their self-regulation of marketing.

Settings that Promote Health

Homes, schools, workplaces, health care establishments and other settings offer opportunities to encourage healthy behaviour, improve social support and strengthen norms and customs that favour lighter drinking. Action to realize this potential includes the training of professionals who work with people in these settings, and the provision of incentives and financial and other support for developing activities in the settings.

Potential Targets

Potential targets for settings for health promotion could focus on:

- the extent of the training for professionals who work with people in these settings;

- the extent of incentives for settings-based activities; and
- the extent of activities in schools, workplaces and municipalities.

Community Action

Community programmes, including informal measures, are an important key to achieving community-wide changes in lifestyles, and to securing political and public support for programmes and policies that manage the sale and use of alcohol *(34)*. In addition, action at the local level makes or at least supports and influences international and national policy. Comprehensive community programmes have been demonstrated to have a positive impact on the control of cardiovascular diseases in Europe *(35)*, and evidence from community programmes on alcohol suggests a similar effect *(36)*.

Potential Target

The potential target regarding community action could focus on:

- the extent of community action programmes.

Safer Alcohol Drinking

Educational programmes can strengthen public support for safer drinking practices. Mass media campaigns against the harm done by alcohol use are important not only because they can affect drinkers but also because they increase public and political support for international and national programmes to manage the sale and use of alcohol *(37,38)*.

The process evaluation of these programmes can be based on information on how they worked. The outcome evaluation can be based on information about the knowledge and attitudes of the people addressed by the programmes.

Potential Targets

Potential targets for safer drinking could focus on:

- the extent and quality of health education activities;
- the extent and quality of mass media campaigns;
- the public's knowledge of the harm done by alcohol use; and

- the public's attitudes to alcohol policy.

Action by the Health Care System

The health care sector, particularly primary health care, should play a leading role in preventing and managing alcohol problems at the local level *(38)*. Primary health care is not just an important setting in which to identify people at risk from heavy drinking and to help them to reduce their consumption. It could also support families and self-help groups and act as an advocate of public health in local communities. A high-risk strategy based on primary health care can complement national and local population-based strategies. Although interventions in general practice have been shown to lead to reductions of around 15% in individuals' alcohol consumption and of around 20% in the proportion of excessive drinkers, compared with control groups, the public health impact of such interventions in isolation is likely to be small *(39)*. The data needed to monitor and evaluate action in primary health care include data on the training of personnel, the activities of the services and the population covered.

The health care sector has the responsibility to provide accessible and appropriate treatment systems, based on the best available evidence *(40)*. Rush *(41)* has offered a useful approach for estimating the required capacity of alcohol treatment services in Canada. The list of service categories that should be considered includes: assessment or referral, detoxification, case management, outpatient treatment, day treatment, short-term residential treatment, long-term residential treatment and after-care.

Rush suggests a four-step systems approach to estimating the required capacity of alcohol treatment services:

1. determining the geographic area and size of the population to be served;
2. estimating the number of problem drinkers and alcohol-dependent drinkers within each population unit (the population in need);
3. estimating the number of individuals from step 2 that should be treated in a given year (the demand population); and
4. estimating the number of individuals from step 3 that will require service from each component of the treatment system.

Potential Targets

Potential targets for health care systems could focus on:

- the extent of preventive activities in primary health care; and
- the availability and accessibility of alcohol treatment services.

Action by the Social Welfare System

The social welfare system in the community is often the first to come into contact with problems associated with alcohol use. It could therefore help to prevent them. The social welfare system could be important not only for identifying and assisting individuals and families at risk from heavy drinking, but also for taking a leading role as welfare advocates in local communities. In the Nordic countries, for example, the social welfare system provides many alcohol treatment services, and is significant in developing settings-based and community action on alcohol.

Potential Targets

Potential targets for the social welfare system could focus on:

- the extent of preventive activities in the social welfare system;
- the availability and accessibility of support and services for families and individuals at risk from high-risk drinking; and
- the availability and accessibility of treatment and counselling services.

Action by the Criminal Justice System

A considerable proportion of the workload of the criminal justice system – in the protection of public and private order, cautions, arrests, sentencing, imprisonment, probation and after-care – relates to alcohol. Effective crime prevention thus gives significant scope for action on alcohol. Partnership between the health and criminal justice systems is needed, for example, in the prevention of drink-driving, domestic violence and unintentional injuries, and in community education.

Potential Targets

Potential targets for the criminal justice system could focus on:

- the extent of preventive activities; and
- the extent of health promotion and health services in prisons.

3

Targets and Indicators for Action at the European Level

Target 17 of the European policy for health for all (see p. 4) calls for a significant reduction in the health-damaging consumption of alcohol. The target text *(3)* further states that the objective is to "reduce alcohol consumption by 25%, with particular attention to reducing harmful use". As mentioned, the attainment of this European target will affect the attainment of the health status targets, will be integrated with the attainment of the lifestyles targets, and will need to be achieved through the principles of the targets for a healthy environment, appropriate care and strategies for health for all development. This also provides a basis for selecting other targets and indicators for alcohol action. The following principles should guide this selection:

- linkage and relevance to other targets in the health policy for Europe;
- measurability and accessibility of data across Member States; and
- relevance to policy across Member States.

These principles of and the experience gained from the regular monitoring and evaluation of progress towards health for all imply that the number of targets and indicators should be small. This would facilitate the obtaining of data from the maximum number of countries. It would also allow annual updating of the data. Thus, we suggest one alcohol use target and three health status targets for use at the European level. We also suggest that, if additional targets are possible, a second alcohol use target and a control policy target be selected. These could be updated periodically, perhaps every 2–5 years. In addition, the WHO Regional Office for Europe periodically collects and analyses other data, which may vary from country to country, to monitor and evaluate action on alcohol at the European level.

MINIMUM SET OF TARGETS AND INDICATORS

Alcohol Use Target and Indicators

In the 1980s, alcohol consumption decreased in one third of Member States, remained stable in one third and increased in the remaining third (see Table 4). When the WHO Regional Committee for Europe first adopted target 17, in 1984, most Member States had experienced a rapid increase in overall alcohol consumption between 1950 and 1980. The target was thus very ambitious. Developments in the 1980s, however, proved that the target is realistic. Some countries with a high baseline level of consumption, such as France and Spain, have a good chance of achieving the target, and Italy has already done so. The countries have also experienced a significant reduction in the number of alcohol-related health problems (see Table 4). While these countries still have comparatively high consumption per head and a further decrease would result in significant health gain, they show that target 17 can be achieved.

Two indicators could be related to this target. The first is recorded alcohol consumption. As discussed, the data can be obtained from various national statistics. Produktschap voor Gedistilleerde Dranken in the Netherlands collates and publishes data from many WHO Member States in its series on world drinking trends *(42)*, and the WHO Regional Office for Europe uses them to indicate the total consumption of alcohol per head. While consumption data are usually presented with the whole population as the denominator, the use of the population over 15 years of age as the denominator is recommended in comparisons of countries in which children under 15 comprise widely different shares of the population. In most countries,

Table 4. Changes in total recorded alcohol consumption and standardized death rates for external causes, road traffic accidents, and chronic liver disease and cirrhosis of the liver in the European Region between 1980 and 1990

Country	Total consumption			Liver disease			External causes			Traffic accidents		
	Litres of pure alcohol per head		Change (%)	Deaths per 100 000		Change (%)	Deaths per 100 000		Change (%)	Deaths per 100 000		Change (%)
	1980	1990		1980	1990		1980	1990		1980	1990	
Armenia	2.4	2.9	+21				48.49[a]	65.57	+35	9.45[a]	21.22	+122
Austria	10.5	11.2	+7	29.24	25.82	–12	85.69	63.36	–26	23.56	16.75	–29
Azerbaijan							56.19[a]	52.46	–7	14.55[a]	16.88	+16
Belarus	10.2	5.7	–44	8.0	6.7	–16	97.6	103.4	+6	15.37[a]	23.21	+51
Belgium	10.8	9.9	–8	12.86	11.28	–12	80.1	57.68	–28	23.76	17.4	–27
Bulgaria	8.7	9.3	+7	10.01	15.97	+60	61.06	60.85	0	12.68	15.51	+22
Croatia		4.1		38.8	31.7	–18	90.3	91.9	+2	28.9	21.2	–27
Czech Republic	9.0	8.9	0					80.6				
Denmark	9.2	9.6	+9	11.35	13.36	+18	71.67	61.67	–14	13.01	10.86	–17
Estonia	11.2	6.0	–47		5.65			130.46			33.16	
Finland	6.4	7.7	+20	6.76	10.59	+57	79.07	90.07	+14	11.65	12.33	+6
France	14.9	12.6	–15	28.88	17.45	–40	85.81	72.04	–16	19.72	16.83	–15
Georgia	7.0	3.4	–51				57.5[a]	58.29	+1	2.98[a]	13.98	+369
Germany					20.02			49.39			12.41	
former German Democratic Republic	10.1	11.8	+17		22.32		37.2	74.56	+100	11.43	18.93	+66

Table 4 (contd)

Country	Total consumption: Litres of pure alcohol per head 1980	Total consumption: Litres of pure alcohol per head 1990	Total consumption: Change (%)	Liver disease: Deaths per 100 000 1980	Liver disease: Deaths per 100 000 1990	Liver disease: Change (%)	External causes: Deaths per 100 000 1980	External causes: Deaths per 100 000 1990	External causes: Change (%)	Traffic accidents: Deaths per 100 000 1980	Traffic accidents: Deaths per 100 000 1990	Traffic accidents: Change (%)
Federal Republic of Germany[b]	11.4	10.6	–7	24.42	19.41	–21	64.54	43.24	–33	18.84	10.77	–43
Greece	6.7	8.6	+28	10.57	8	–24	47.23	40.45	–14	16.85	20.96	+24
Hungary	11.8	10.8	+8	27.39	50.66	+85	114.29	121.19	+6	15.77	24.39	+55
Iceland	3.9	3.9	0	0.94	1.11	+18	66.3	51.4	–22	9.54	9.77	+2
Ireland	7.3	7.2	–1	4.73	2.65	–44	54.52	44.41	–19	17.14	13.23	–23
Israel	1	1	0	10.93	8.68	–21	41.2	50.88	+23	11.72	8.41	–28
Italy	13	9.0	–31	32.89	22.6	–31	54.07	43.38	–20	18.64	14.36	–23
Kazakhstan							120.7[a]	114.64	–5	15.89[a]	23.35	+47
Kyrgyzstan		2.8					99.79[a]	112.16	+12	24.58[a]	27.21	+11
Latvia	11.3	5.3	–53				145.59[a]	138.32	–5	28.05[a]	38.82	+38
Lithuania	11.1	5.0	–55		8.1		138.7[a]	122.23	–12	24.7[a]	30.81	+25
Luxembourg	10.9	12.2	+12	23.01	23.65	+3	86.59	58.4	–33	28.53	17.4	–39
Malta				12.68	11.94	–6	44.19	30.35	–31	8.13	1.62	–80
Netherlands	8.8	8.1	–8	5.1	4.83	–5	43	32.28	–25	12.71	8.07	–37
Norway	4.6	4.1	–11	5.82	5.38	–8	60.57	54.21	–11	8.66	7.43	–14
Poland	8.7	6.2	–29	14.41	11.43	–21	80.69	82.47	+2		22.43	
Portugal	10	10.1	+1	33.23	24.54	–26	75.11	66.37	–12	28.02	26.92	–4

Table 4 (contd)

Country	Total consumption: Litres of pure alcohol per head 1980	1990	Change (%)	Liver disease: Deaths per 100 000 1980	1990	Change (%)	External causes: Deaths per 100 000 1980	1990	Change (%)	Traffic accidents: Deaths per 100 000 1980	1990	Change (%)
Republic of Moldova	6.8	3.3	–51	79.3	68.1	–14	120.68[a]	112.09	–7	25.28[a]	29.8	+18
Romania	8	7.6	–5	32.7	34.6	+6	70.25	79.36	+13		19.53	
Russian Federation	10.5	5.6	–47	11.5	9.4	–18	157.15[a]	135.68	–14	18.77[a]	24.42	+30
Slovakia	10.7	10.4	–3	36.43	44.3	+22	67.0	74.0	+10	10.69	12.49	+17
Slovenia	11.9	10.2	–14		34			67.6			21.7	
Spain	13.6	10.8	–21	24.18	19.34	–20	42.94	46.76	+7	16.76	19.31	+15
Sweden	5.7	5.5	–4	11.17	6.51	–42	62.74	51.85	–17	10.37	8.16	–21
Switzerland	10.8	10.8	0	12.55	9.31	–26	72.96	66.38	–9	18.17	12.8	–30
Tajikistan							51.46[a]	56.85	+10	13.68[a]	17.46	+31
The Former Yugoslav Republic of Macedonia	2.0	3.5	+75							16.3	10.7	–34
Turkey	0.7	0.7	0									
Turkmenistan	4.3	2.7	–37	20.9	19.74	–2	61.2	66.77	+9	18.8	20.69	+10
Ukraine	6.3	4.1	–35				107.5[a]	107.38	0	15.03[a]	22.96	+53
United Kingdom	7.3	7.6	+4	4.6	5.98	+30	41.08	33.26	–19	11.31	9.06	–20
former USSR	6.2	3.7	–40					118.67			23.37	

Table 4 (contd)

Country	Total consumption			Liver disease			External causes			Traffic accidents		
	Litres of pure alcohol per head		Change (%)	Deaths per 100 000		Change (%)	Deaths per 100 000		Change (%)	Deaths per 100 000		Change (%)
	1980	1990		1980	1990		1980	1990		1980	1990	
Uzbekistan							72.81[a]	71.06	–2	13.57[a]	19.74	+45
former Yugoslavia	7.8	6.6	–15	24	18.01	–25	66.88	61.21	–8	22.74	16.85	–26
EU average	11.41	9.91	–13	21.39	15.9	–26	58.94	47.67	–19	17.39	14.1	–19
European Region average	10.44	9.18	–12	20.62	17.45	–15	63.4	57.13	–10	16.92	14.42	–15

[a] Figure for 1981 rather than 1980.

[b] Before the accession of the German Democratic Republic.

Note: The table covers all countries on which WHO had data.

Source: Health for all database of the WHO Regional Office for Europe.

children either do not drink alcoholic beverages or consume insignificant amounts.

The second indicator is the estimated sum of recorded and unrecorded alcohol consumption. In many countries home production, unrecorded imports by travellers, and untaxed or other illegally sold alcohol comprise a significant part of total consumption. Estimates of the volume of unrecorded consumption can be based on the information given by the police and the customs authorities, the demand for raw materials and technology for home production, and surveys of drinking habits that address this issue *(43)*. In the absence of reliable estimates of unrecorded alcohol consumption, recorded consumption alone may be used with due caution.

Potential Target and Indicators

A potential target on alcohol use could call for:

- alcohol consumption per head to be reduced by 25%.

Potential indicators could be:

- recorded total consumption of alcohol per head; and
- the sum of recorded and estimated unrecorded total consumption of alcohol per head.

Health Status Targets and Indicators

Out of many possible targets on alcohol-related damage to health, three targets on alcohol-related mortality are suggested. They are: mortality from liver cirrhosis, injuries and alcohol-related road traffic accidents. The selection of these targets is based on their public health significance, their measurability, the accessibility of data and the importance of alcohol as a contributory or determining factor. The WHO Regional Office for Europe collects data related to all three for its health for all database; some of these data are given in Table 4.

In addition, many countries collect data on such topics as mortality and morbidity from alcohol dependence and alcoholic psychosis. The definitions and diagnostic criteria for these conditions vary, however, and changes in treatment provision influence the morbidity data.

Liver Cirrhosis

Liver cirrhosis remains the most important health indicator. Temporal and regional correlations between alcohol consumption and liver cirrhosis are very high *(44)*. A fall in alcohol consumption almost always leads to a fall in the death rate from cirrhosis and other chronic liver disease. Other factors also come into play: there would be some time-lag in death rates from cirrhosis, some deaths are not caused by alcohol, and improved treatment could decrease the death rates further *(45)*. Nevertheless, in most countries and at most times, changes in liver cirrhosis mortality reflect changes in total alcohol consumption and in the number of many other alcohol-related problems. The subtarget on liver cirrhosis calls for a reduction of 25%, the same figure as that for alcohol consumption.

Injuries

In a number of countries, injuries (including those that are unintentional and those due to violent behaviour) are an important cause of death, and the most important cause of years of life lost before the age of 65 *(20)*. Motor vehicle deaths account for about half the deaths from injuries. Falls, drowning, fires and violence are other important causes of death *(46,47)*. Injuries incapacitate many more people, with many suffering life-long disabilities. Injuries generate huge costs in lost productivity and medical care.

Injuries comprise a family of complex problems involving many different areas of society. Reducing them requires the involvement of many sectors, including health, education, transportation, law, engineering, architecture and safety sciences.

Nevertheless, alcohol use is associated with both the causes and the severity of many injuries and may be related to between one third and one half of all injury deaths *(46)*. Target 11 of the health for all policy calls for a reduction of at least 25% in the injuries, disabilities and deaths arising from accidents. The suggested alcohol target, which addresses homicide and purposeful injuries in addition to accidents, accordingly aims at the same numerical decrease.

Alcohol-related Road Traffic Accidents

The proportion of deaths in road traffic accidents that are related to alcohol is decreasing in a number of countries. This could be attributed to the emergence of highly visible citizens' groups, the attention that they attract from the mass media, and the resulting increases in activities to deter drinking and driving. These involve the making and better enforcement of laws and the more frequent use of sanctions such as the suspending and revoking of driving licences *(48)*.

A target on this topic could address deaths caused by road traffic accidents because of the availability of reliable and precise data. While injuries are also a serious problem, the data are not as good. Decreases in deaths may indicate parallel reductions in injuries, but improvements in occupant protection and emergency medical services may prevent deaths while the incidence of injuries actually increases. In general, the surveillance of injuries caused by road traffic accidents needs improvement.

A target on traffic accidents is more difficult to attain in countries with rapid increases in the number of private cars. Nevertheless, experience from many countries proves that the number of alcohol-related traffic deaths can be decreased, even when the total consumption of alcohol changes only slightly. Thus, the numerical target could have a more ambitious goal than a 25% reduction.

Many countries collect data on alcohol-related traffic deaths, and have studied the role of alcohol in them and in all accidents. In the absence of continuously collected data on alcohol-related deaths, these studies can be used to make estimates. The WHO health for all database does not yet include data on deaths from alcohol-related road traffic accidents.

Potential Targets and Indicators

Potential targets on health status could call for:

- the death rate for cirrhosis of the liver to be reduced by 25%;
- the death rate for injury to be reduced by at least 25%; and
- the death rate from alcohol-related road traffic accidents to be reduced by 33%.

Potential indicators could be:

- standardized death rate from cirrhosis of the liver and chronic liver disease per 100 000 population;
- standardized death rate from external causes of injury and poisoning per 100 000 population; and
- standardized death rate from road traffic accidents related to alcohol per 100 000 population.

ADDITIONAL TARGETS AND INDICATORS

About half of the Member States of the European Region have already provided the WHO health for all database with data on the indicators on recorded alcohol use and health status. Table 4 shows not only that the subtargets are realistic but also that events in countries can lead to widely different figures on changes in the levels given. In Spain, for example, an increase in traffic may explain the increase in injuries and traffic accidents, while the share of alcohol-related accidents may have decreased. In some countries, unrecorded alcohol consumption may have taken a larger share of total consumption, but figures on recorded consumption do not reflect this change.

As Table 4 shows, Italy has already achieved the targets on alcohol consumption, road traffic accidents and chronic liver disease and cirrhosis, and is close to achieving the target on injuries. Italy and the other countries close to a 25% reduction in consumption had comparatively high baseline levels of total alcohol consumption and related health problems. Thus, they are expected to aim at further reductions in consumption. Their experience with such work may be useful in developing objectives and policies on high-risk drinking. If the countries with much lower baseline levels of alcohol use also attain the target on consumption, the next step is to discuss additional targets.

The minimum targets and indicators have two major shortcomings. They do not address either the harmful use mentioned in target 17 or alcohol policy. Thus, two additional targets should deal with these issues.

Harmful Alcohol Use

Regular heavy drinking and intoxication can be described as harmful alcohol use, but there is no clear definition of the term.

The International Classification of Diseases (ICD), developed by WHO in collaboration with leading research centres of the world, helps to improve the accuracy and international comparability of mortality and morbidity data. In particular, the tenth revision (ICD-10) has improved the classification of and the criteria for mental and behavioural disorders related to alcohol. It defines harmful use as a pattern of alcohol use that causes damage to physical or mental health *(49)*. This excludes, however, a level of consumption that places a person at risk of health damage. The risk of a number of physical problems (cirrhosis, stroke and certain types of cancer) significantly increases when consumption exceeds 20 g pure alcohol per day for both men and women *(23)*.

Targets could therefore be adopted to reduce the proportion of the population with such consumption levels. Changes in consumption per head have been shown to result from changes in the drinking habits of people at all levels of consumption. High-risk drinkers change their drinking habits in the same direction and by roughly the same percentage, according to many studies *(50,22)*. Because service provision and, in some countries, education campaigns are aimed at reducing alcohol consumption among high-risk drinkers, it may be possible to set a higher target for this group than that for reductions in consumption per head. Such a target, however, could be too ambitious. The studies that have proved the relationship between drinking levels for the population and the prevalence of heavy drinking also indicate that a larger reduction in the latter is very difficult to achieve.

ICD-10 *(49)* defines acute intoxication as "a transient condition following the administration of alcohol . . . resulting in disturbances in level of consciousness, cognition, perception, affect or behaviour, or other psychophysiological functions and responses". A WHO test to identify alcohol use disorders *(51)* includes a question on the frequency of heavy drinking: "How often do you have six or more drinks on one occasion?". In particular, the risk for accidents and other injuries is greatly increased in the state of intoxication. Targets could therefore be adopted to reduce the occasions for drinking that lead to intoxication.

While most countries have no routinely collected data to indicate the frequency of intoxication or the prevalence of heavy drinking, some conduct regular surveys of the drinking habits of representative samples of the population. Many of these surveys provide enough information to monitor changes in the prevalence of heavy drinking. For instance, the Finnish surveys estimate the frequency of intoxication *(11)*.

Heavy drinking has attracted more interest, however. More countries use methodologies to estimate its prevalence (see Annex 2), and it might be easier to agree on a minimum standard methodology for this task. Some countries, such as the United Kingdom *(52)* and the United States *(5)*, have already set targets to reduce heavy drinking. This is thus the subject of the proposed additional target on alcohol use. To monitor and evaluate the attainment of this target, more countries should regularly survey drinking habits, using a minimum standardized methodology to estimate the prevalence of heavy drinking.

Potential Target and Indicator

A potential target on harmful alcohol use could call for:

- the proportion of individuals who consume in excess of 20 g pure alcohol a day (for both men and women) to be reduced by 25%.

A potential indicator could be:

- the prevalence of heavy drinking, based on data from surveys of drinking habits.

Alcohol Control Policies

Some potential objectives are available for improved public health policies on alcohol. We suggest focusing on alcohol control policies owing to the comparability and accessibility of the relevant data.

Davies & Walsh *(53)* developed a preliminary scale to estimate the comprehensiveness of an alcohol control policy. The scale included a list of 30 potential policy options; these comprise options 1–30 in the suggested European scale of alcohol control policy shown in Table 5. Each policy option is worth 1 point and no attempt is made to give certain policy options more weight than others. Thus, a country can have a minimum score of 0 and a maximum of 30 points on Davies & Walsh's scale. Even such a rough measure of the comprehensiveness of alcohol control policy seems to be a useful means of monitoring. For instance, Table 6 shows that Italy, Spain and France have been the most active in introducing new policy options *(54)*. They are also the countries that showed the greatest decreases in overall alcohol consumption in the 1980s.

The suggested European scale has more policy options, covering random breath testing of drivers, warning labels on alcohol products, restrictions on the maximum alcohol content of beverages and bans on advertising. It is also sensitive to differences in the enforcement of alcohol control legislation.

If the suggested scale is adopted, collecting data from countries to calculate their scores would be a simple task. This would permit the setting of a realistic maximum score for all the Member States in the Region to achieve by the year 2000.

Potential Target and Indicator

A potential target on alcohol control policies could call for:

- all Member States to obtain a score of 17 or more on the European scale of alcohol control policy.

A potential indicator could be:

- the score on the European scale of alcohol control policy.

Table 5. A European scale of alcohol control policy

	Policy options
1.	National alcohol prevention agency(ies)
2.	National alcohol education programmes
3.	Legislation on alcohol-free settings
4.	Drinking and driving: blood alcohol concentration (any)
5.	Drinking and driving: blood alcohol concentration of 50 mg per 100 ml or lower
6.	Drinking and driving penalty: automatic suspension of driving licence
7.	Drinking and driving penalty: automatic imprisonment
8.	Alcohol taxation on wines
9.	Alcohol taxation on beers
10.	Alcohol taxation on spirits
11.	Annual adjustment of taxation on wines
12.	Annual adjustment of taxation on beers
13.	Annual adjustment of taxation on spirits
14.	Maintenance of or increase in real price of alcoholic beverages
15.	Restrictions on hours and days of sale or serving
16.	Restrictions on the density of outlets
17.	Restrictions on the type and location of outlets
18.	Restrictions on the age for sale and serving (16 years)
19.	Restrictions on the age for sale and serving (18 years)
20.	Restrictions on the age for sale and serving (20 years)
21.	Restrictions on alcohol advertising: voluntary code
22.	Restrictions on alcohol advertising: statutory controls
23.	Licence required for the production of alcoholic beverages
24.	State monopoly for the distribution of spirits
25.	State monopoly for the distribution of wines
26.	State monopoly for the distribution of beers
27.	State monopoly for spirits production
28.	State monopoly for wine production
29.	State monopoly for beer production
30.	Allocation of part of a monopoly's profits for the prevention and/or treatment of alcohol-related harm
31.	Frequent use of random breath testing of car drivers
32.	Mandatory warning labels on alcohol products
33.	Restrictions on the maximum alcohol content of beverages
34.	Ban on alcohol product advertising on television
35.	Ban on alcohol product advertising on other common media
36.	Effective enforcement of control of production
37.	Effective enforcement of control of distribution

Source: adapted from Davies & Walsh *(53)*.

Table 6. The scores of some European countries on the Davies & Walsh scale of alcohol control policy, 1981 and 1991

Country	Score	
	1981	1991
Norway	27	23
Sweden	24	21
Poland	20	18
United Kingdom	16	17
Ireland	15	16
France	12	15
Switzerland	14	14
Denmark	14	13
Belgium	11	13
Italy	9	12
Spain	6	10
Federal Republic of Germany[a]	12	9
Netherlands	9	9
Austria	6	8
Luxembourg	5	8
Average	13.3	13.7

[a] Before the accession of the German Democratic Republic.

Source: Contel *(54)*.

EUROPEAN SUMMARIES ON ALCOHOL, DRUGS AND TOBACCO

The WHO Regional Office for Europe will periodically collect, analyse and publish a summary of data on problems, policies and programmes related to alcohol, drugs and tobacco in the European Region. These summaries will include monitoring and evaluation based on the targets and indicators described above. They will also use other data from monitoring and evaluations by countries. The summaries should also address the trade in alcohol within and outside the European Region. They should contain information about new trends in alcohol consumption and problems, innovations in prevention and treatment, subregional comparisons and examples of good practice. WHO has already issued separate summaries on alcohol *(2)*, drugs *(55)* and tobacco *(56)*.

4

Targets and Indicators for Action at the National Level

A few countries, such as Sweden *(57)* and the United Kingdom *(52)*, have developed and others are developing national health strategies that include objectives, targets and indicators related to action on alcohol. More countries have monitoring and reporting systems for such action *(2,58–62)*.

Targets for the national level should be selected according to the availability of reliable indicators, as well as their relevance to the attainment of the main targets on health status. This chapter therefore begins by discussing indicators of alcohol use, health status and policy. It concludes with a short discussion about the setting of national targets and indicators, the evaluation of qualitative changes and the frequency of monitoring and evaluation.

ALCOHOL USE INDICATORS

Indicators of alcohol use should allow the monitoring and evaluation of trends in overall consumption, high-risk consumption and the consumption patterns of different population groups.

Consumption per Head

The same indicators of alcohol consumption per head may be used at the European and national levels. If unrecorded consumption can be expected to comprise a relatively stable share of overall consumption, data on recorded consumption are sufficient for annual monitoring. The share of unrecorded consumption, however, should be estimated every 5–8 years. Because rapid changes in the alcohol market may affect this share, countries experiencing such changes should produce estimates more frequently.

Potential Indicators

Potential indicators could be:

- the recorded total alcohol consumption per head; and
- the sum of recorded and estimated unrecorded total alcohol consumption per head.

High-risk Consumption

The health and social welfare authorities and the police, who treat or control alcohol-related problems, can give some indication of trends in the prevalence of high-risk drinking. Their information, however, covers only an unknown proportion of high-risk drinkers. In addition to the frequency and prevalence of high-risk drinking, other factors may explain changes in the number of high-risk drinkers in contact with the authorities. As mentioned, a decrease in the numbers treated for alcohol dependence, for example, may reflect a decrease in prevalence, a cut in services or a change in the division of work within the services.

National surveys comprise the best available methodology to estimate the prevalence and frequency of high-risk drinking. They also provide information on drinking habits by sex, age and occupational and socioeconomic group.

Different types of general population surveys focus on particular groups, such as schoolchildren and students, and contain questions related to alcohol consumption. Only the surveys that use similar methodology and questions and are repeated at reasonable intervals provide data for indicators, because the data can be used to analyse changes in consumption (see Annex 2).

Surveys that may provide data on alcohol consumption include those on:

- particular drinking habits *(11)*;
- households *(9)*;
- household budgets and consumption *(10)*;
- health interviews *(63)*;
- the health behaviour of school-age children *(16)*; and
- other topics, including market research if the methodology is adequate *(15)*.

Depending on the available survey data, different indicators may be developed. They should address the most frequent and most serious types of high-risk consumption.

Potential Indicators

Potential indicators for high-risk consumption, based on survey data, could be:

- the prevalence of drinking in excess of 20 g pure alcohol a day by men and women in different age groups;
- the frequency of drinking leading to intoxication in different age groups; and
- the prevalence of drinking in groups below the minimum legal drinking age.

HEALTH STATUS INDICATORS

The same minimum set of health status indicators can be used at the European and national levels: mortality from liver cirrhosis, injuries and alcohol-related traffic accidents. In most countries, other indicators, based on either mortality or morbidity data, can also be used.

In principle, the indicators could include all the conditions in which alcohol is estimated to account for 25% or more of deaths (see Table 2). The greater the role of alcohol, the more probable that changes in the mortality and morbidity from a condition reflect changes in alcohol use. Other criteria for selecting conditions as indicators are their public health impact and the accuracy with which they are diagnosed.

For instance, mortality from alcohol-related cancer meets the second and third criteria. Mortality and morbidity from alcoholic psychosis, alcohol dependence and alcohol withdrawal syndrome meet the first and second, but it might be better to use the combined figures for these three conditions because diagnoses may not distinguish between them very accurately. Alcoholic cardiomyopathy can only be used if diagnostic accuracy in the country is estimated to be high enough. In addition, some countries have used mortality and morbidity from acute and chronic pancreatitis and alcohol poisoning as indicators *(60,61)*.

As mentioned in Chapter 3, ICD-10 *(49)* has improved the classification of mental and behavioural disorders related to alcohol. Nevertheless, the use of morbidity statistics that are based on the treatment of these conditions is suggested only if the impact of structural, quantitative and qualitative changes in the provision of treatment are taken into consideration when presenting the data.

Most of these data can also be used to create indicators for certain population groups, determined by age, sex, ethnicity, socioeconomic status or geographical location. Such indicators can be useful. For example, mortality statistics for age groups permit an estimate of the years of life lost due to different alcohol-related diseases, and thus the setting of targets to decrease this number.

Potential Indicators

Potential indicators for health status, based on mortality and morbidity statistics, could be:

- the death rate from cirrhosis of the liver, by sex;
- the death rate from road traffic accidents or from those related to alcohol (if available);

- the death rate from external causes of injury and poisoning, by sex and age;
- the death rate from homicide and purposeful injury, by sex and age;
- the death rate from cancer of the lip, oral cavity, pharynx, oesophagus and larynx, by sex and age;
- the death rate from alcoholic psychosis, alcohol dependence and alcohol withdrawal syndrome, by sex and age;
- the death rate from alcohol poisoning, particularly for young people;
- the death rate from pancreatitis, by sex and age;
- hospital admissions for pancreatitis, liver cirrhosis and alcohol-related injuries; and
- admissions to inpatient treatment for alcoholic psychosis, alcohol dependence and alcohol withdrawal syndrome, by sex and age.

The countries that collect data for these indicators usually do so annually. This provides opportunities for monitoring at short intervals.

SOCIAL AND ECONOMIC INDICATORS

Social Problems

The role of alcohol in many social problems makes the monitoring and evaluation of the impact of alcohol action on these problems an important task.

Most of the available data are based on the activities of social welfare and criminal justice authorities for alleviation, and may thus reflect the level of these activities more than the prevalence and frequency of the problems. If one takes this bias into consideration when presenting the data, there are many opportunities to create social problem indicators at the national level.

The data sources, problem definitions and statistical classifications vary widely between countries. Thus, we do not suggest concrete indicators but only data that could be used to create them. This means, unfortunately, that the international comparability of these data and indicators based on them is rather low.

Data for Potential Indicators

Data for indicators of potential social problems could include those on:

- child abuse;
- family violence;
- the cause of divorces;
- homelessness related to alcohol use;
- financial problems of private persons and families related to alcohol use;
- police cautions and arrests for disturbing public order;
- drink-driving; and
- crime committed while intoxicated.

Many of these data allow indicators that refer to people in different sex, age and socioeconomic groups and geographic locations.

Economic Indicators

Many of the indicators and data described above may be used to show the economic costs of alcohol-related problems. This will underline the gains that could be obtained by prevention and health promotion.

In addition, some economic data are of great importance for the evaluation of alcohol policy. General household surveys *(9,10)* may produce data on the share of family budgets used for purchasing alcohol. The price index of alcoholic beverages may be compared with that of other or all consumer goods. These data give an important insight into the role of alcohol in the household economy, and thus into the impact of changes in alcohol consumption and alcohol policies on people's economic wellbeing.

Developments in the state revenue from alcohol, including that from tax and excise and possible state enterprises, do not directly reflect trends in alcohol consumption. In most countries, a moderate increase in taxes on alcohol could simultaneously increase state revenue and decrease consumption *(28)*. Monitoring might be necessary to show that only a small proportion (1–2% in most countries) of the revenue from alcohol taxes would cover all the costs of national programmes to prevent alcohol-related harm.

In addition, the costs of alcohol-related problems to employers can be estimated. These include absenteeism due to alcohol-related problems, alcohol-related accidents at work, and the sickness and pension insurance costs due to alcohol-related diseases.

Data for Potential Indicators

Data for potential economic indicators could come from:

- studies estimating the economic costs of alcohol-related health and social problems;
- price indices for alcoholic beverages and other consumer goods;
- general household surveys that cover purchases of alcohol as part of the overall household budget;
- statistics on state revenue from tax and excise on alcohol and from possible state alcohol enterprises; and
- studies estimating the economic costs of alcohol-related problems to employers.

ALCOHOL POLICY INDICATORS

Monitoring and evaluation of alcohol policies require qualitative and quantitative data to answer many questions, such as whether:

- the overall policy is comprehensive enough and policy measures known to be effective are used;
- legislation is effectively enforced;
- the authorities responsible for implementing the policies obtain sufficient training and other support;

- the policies reach the target populations; and
- the target populations have benefited from the policies as expected.

National Policies for Alcohol Control

The suggested European scale of alcohol control policy (Table 5) gives a rough estimate of the comprehensiveness of national alcohol control policy. At the national level, more detailed description and evaluation may be needed. The options for alcohol control policy are discussed extensively in the second publication in the series of the European Alcohol Action Plan *(31)*. Most of the evaluation can be made without additional indicators, because the outcome of control policy can be monitored and evaluated through those on alcohol use, health status and social factors. For many countries, the estimated unrecorded alcohol consumption per head is an important indicator to evaluate the effectiveness of the enforcement of legislation.

Potential Indicators

Potential indicators for alcohol control policy could be:

- the score on the European scale of alcohol control policy;
- estimated unrecorded alcohol consumption per head; and
- indicators of health status and social problems.

Supportive Environments

The options for developing alcohol action by municipalities and in other everyday environments are discussed in the fifth publication of the European Alcohol Action Plan series *(64)*. The potential indicators measure the proportion of these settings for which adequate action has been developed and the proportion of the population found in the settings.

Adequate action should be defined on the basis of available information. It may mean the training of teachers or occupational health staff, a written, adopted alcohol programme in municipalities or enterprises, or a survey of alcohol policies in various settings.

Potential Indicators

Potential indicators for monitoring supportive environments could be:

- the proportion of municipalities (cities, towns and villages) with an alcohol policy or programme and the proportion of the total population living in those municipalities;
- the proportion of workplaces with an adequate alcohol policy and the proportion of all employees working there;
- the proportion of schools giving adequate skills education on alcohol and the proportion of pupils covered; and
- the proportion of municipalities with adequate alcohol action and the proportion of the total population living in those communities.

Education Programmes

As the objective of most education programmes is to change the behaviour of the target group, the ultimate aim of those on alcohol is to secure a positive change or prevent a negative change in drinking patterns. Education programmes very seldom have so large an impact on drinking patterns that it can be distinguished from that of other influences *(37)*. Thus, changes in knowledge about and attitudes towards alcohol and alcohol policies are better indicators of the impact of education programmes. Data for these indicators may be available from routine population and opinion surveys.

Potential Indicators

Potential indicators for the monitoring and evaluation of educational programmes could be:

- the public's knowledge about harm done by alcohol use; and
- the public's knowledge about services to support individuals to prevent and manage alcohol-related problems.

ATTITUDES TO ALCOHOL AND ALCOHOL CONTROL POLICIES

Action by the Health, Social Welfare and Criminal Justice Systems

It is rather difficult to monitor the extent to which the staff of the health, social welfare and criminal justice systems implement national guidelines for preventing and managing alcohol-related problems. Information can be obtained, however, on the training given to staff and the inclusion of particular prevention programmes in the work plans of local services. For instance, a WHO working group *(65)* suggested that information be collected at the national level on the role of primary health care physicians in preventing and managing the harm done by alcohol use:

- the extent of mandatory or optional education on alcohol in medical training;
- the estimated percentage of primary health care physicians who specialize in treating alcohol problems;
- the estimated percentage of physicians who routinely assess patients' risk of alcohol problems; and
- the existence of policy statements on alcohol by the physicians' national organizations.

Potential Indicators

Potential indicators for the monitoring and evaluation of action by the health, social welfare and criminal justice systems to prevent and manage alcohol-related problems could be:

- the proportion of health care staff who have received basic education in prevention and management;
- the proportion of health care staff who have acquired an agreed minimum of skills to provide prevention and management services;
- the proportion of primary health care units that offer preventive services and the proportion of the population covered;

- the proportion of general hospitals that provide appropriate prevention and management services;
- the proportion of staff in the social welfare system who have received appropriate education in prevention and management; and
- the proportion of staff in the criminal justice system who have received appropriate education in prevention and management.

Treatment Services

A systems approach to evaluate the treatment services for alcohol-related problems was presented earlier (see p.28). Some of the health status indicators may also be used to evaluate the accessibility and impact of treatment services. For example, better outreach activities, services for the homeless and detoxification services might decrease a high death rate from alcohol poisoning, alcoholic psychosis and alcohol dependence.

Potential Indicators

Potential indicators for alcohol treatment services could be:

- the availability of assessment or referral services, detoxification, case management, outpatient treatment, day treatment, short-term residential treatment, long-term residential treatment and after-care;
- the availability of self-help groups, such as Alcoholics Anonymous and groups for members of the families of alcohol-dependent persons;
- the accessibility of various treatment services and self-help groups; and
- mortality from alcohol poisoning, alcoholic psychosis and alcohol dependence.

EVALUATION AND MONITORING AT THE NATIONAL LEVEL

There are many potential national targets and indicators for alcohol action. Both the leadership in alcohol policy and the monitoring of the policy's impact could be more effective if only a few, most important targets are selected. We suggest that all countries adopt the targets and indicators proposed for the European level. Many countries could need additional national targets that address the most serious problems or the policies that most need development in the near future. Countries may also use many additional indicators and types of data, perhaps more infrequently, as a part of the monitoring and evaluation process.

Evaluation cannot be based on targets and indicators alone. It should also use other types of knowledge and address other types of questions. These may include the following.

Survey data should be used to reveal people's motives for drinking and for restricting drinking, experience with alcohol-related problems, contexts of drinking and other issues related to drinking habits. These factors may be significant in developing and focusing alcohol policies. In addition, public discussion of alcohol use and related problems, and policies and surveys on people's attitudes towards and opinions on alcohol policies, may be significant in evaluating what effective policies are politically feasible and on which problems the policies should particularly focus.

Evaluation should also address the experiences of professionals and other staff working for the implementation of the policy at the local level. Such people may notice important changes in consumption and problems that are not yet reflected in national statistics. In addition, they should give feedback on the successes and problems of policy implementation.

Comparisons with other countries may point out deficiencies, problems or opportunities that would otherwise remain unnoticed.

Finally, the evaluation process should consider explanations for changes in the indicators other than the impact of alcohol policy, such as changes in social structures or drinking cultures.

Potential Targets

A basic set of potential targets at the national level could call for:

- a reduction in the consumption of alcohol per head;
- a reduction in the proportion of high-risk drinkers;
- a reduction in the death rate from cirrhosis of the liver;
- a reduction in the death rate from injuries;
- a reduction in the death rate from alcohol-related road traffic accidents;
- a reduction in other monitored alcohol-related deaths;
- a reduction in the need for alcohol treatment;
- a reduction in alcohol-related social problems;
- the introduction of a more comprehensive alcohol policy;
- an increase in the number of settings in which adequate alcohol action is taken;
- an increase in the public's knowledge about alcohol and support for alcohol policy;
- an increase in the proportion of professional staff trained for alcohol action; and
- improved accessibility of alcohol treatment services.

5

Targets and Indicators for Action at the Local Level

More and more subnational regions and cities have developed their own health strategies *(63,66)*, many of which include targets for alcohol consumption and related problems *(67)*. Some regions and many cities *(68)* have adopted action plans on alcohol. The European Alcohol Action Plan *(3)* advocates action at the local level, where the adoption of targets and the monitoring of their attainment with indicators has proved to be effective *(67)*.

Many of the targets and indicators for the national level may also be applied at the local level. For example, the targets on alcohol use, health status and social problems may be the same at both levels. Some aspects of alcohol policy, such as taxation or restricting marketing in national mass media, however, cannot be decided at the local level.

Many social problems and types of risk behaviour related to alcohol are better known at the local level. It might be possible to create particular targets referring to the areas with the most problems. Particular tasks can be defined for different sectors and units of the public administration. The role of community action, schools, workplaces, local media and nongovernmental organizations can be defined in more detail than at the national level. The local policy might include targets on the serving of alcoholic beverages at events held by the local administration, the serving and advertising of alcoholic beverages during sports, cultural and other events funded totally or partially by the public authorities or held on public premises, and the conditions for the licences issued to and contracts made with local producers and retailers of alcoholic beverages. Some targets can address very specific problems that should be reduced in a short time.

AVAILABILITY OF DATA

In many countries, most of the data on alcohol consumption and related problems and policies are available at the local level. For example, data from the local level on the demand for alcohol treatment, alcohol-related social problems and local alcohol policies are very often more reliable and easier to use. The City of Copenhagen used the following indicators to compare the "alcohol profile" of the city to that of the rest of Denmark *(69)*:

- self-reported alcohol consumption (none, 1–4 units or 5 units or more) on ordinary weekdays and during weekends, by sex (from survey data);
- treatment at outpatient clinics for alcohol abuse;
- treatment for alcoholic psychosis and alcoholism at psychiatric wards and inpatient clinics;
- treatments at general hospitals for alcoholic psychosis, alcoholism, alcohol poisoning, liver cirrhosis and pancreatitis;
- mortality from alcoholic psychosis, alcoholism, alcohol poisoning, liver cirrhosis and pancreatitis;
- arrests for drunkenness and numbers of intoxicated people taken into police custody; and
- the numbers of alcohol licences and of licences with extended opening hours.

Some of the national data are probably not available for use at the local level. Nevertheless, the numbers of alcohol-related health problems and alcohol-related costs to public services and to employers at the local level can be estimated by extrapolation from the national figures. While such estimates are valuable in illustrating the level of the problems, they cannot be used as indicators for local targets. Table 7 gives an example of such extrapolation in the United Kingdom *(70)*.

Table 7. The estimated number of deaths attributable to alcohol in the population over 15 years in Oxford (population 116 000), 1986

Cause	Total deaths in Oxford	Deaths attributable to alcohol in the United Kingdom (%)	Deaths attributable to alcohol in Oxford
Cancer	262	3.5	9
Stroke	112	6.4	7
Respiratory disease	97	6.6	6
Digestive disease (excluding chronic liver disease)	34	6.4	2
Chronic liver disease	5	80.0	4
Injuries and poisonings	38	40.0	15
Other	517	3.3	17
Total	1065	5.6	60

Source: Oxford City Council *(70)*.

In the European Region, alcohol use and related problems often vary more between different areas of a country than between countries. Thus, the baseline data and indicators for local targets should be determined by better methods than simple extrapolation.

MAPPING DATA AT THE SUBLOCAL LEVEL

Some data can be available for the districts or postal code areas of a city. They can be used to set specific targets for and to focus health promotion on the locations in most need. Such data could include those on:

- alcohol consumption (from local surveys);
- mortality and morbidity;

- alcohol-related public order problems, accidents, family violence and crime;
- the density of alcohol retail sale outlets;
- alcohol action at schools and by primary health care; and
- the availability and accessibility of alcohol treatment.

DAILY EXPERIENCE OF LOCAL PEOPLE AND PROFESSIONALS

At the local level in particular, alcohol consumption and related problems and responses mean more than numbers and information collected by other people. They are part of the daily experience of local people and professionals. Some of the local targets can be much more concrete than those at the national level, and address problems that local people see and feel in their daily life. Thus, both the setting of targets and the monitoring of their attainment should directly involve the people who are the subjects and beneficiaries of the policy. Open discussions of targets and as a method of monitoring are necessary parts of community involvement and empowerment in action on alcohol.

POTENTIAL TARGETS

A set of potential targets at the local level could call for:

- a reduction in the consumption of alcohol per head;
- a reduction in the proportion of high-risk drinkers;
- a reduction in locally monitored deaths related to alcohol;
- a reduction in the need for alcohol treatment;
- a reduction in alcohol-related social problems;
- a reduction in alcohol-related problems in particular locations and groups;
- an increase in the number of schools, workplaces and health service units in which adequate alcohol action is taken;

- an increase in the proportion of professional staff trained for alcohol action;
- improvement in the accessibility and quality of alcohol treatment services;
- the development of policies on alcohol for events organized or funded by public authorities or held on public premises;
- the development of policy on the local alcohol and hospitality industry; and
- support for alcohol action by nongovernmental organizations.

6

Conclusion

Setting concrete targets for action is an important step in creating consensus on and political support for the basic aims of public health policy on alcohol. It also helps to link alcohol policy with the overall health strategies at the local, national and international levels. Alcohol action contributes to the attainment of many health status targets and should be linked with the development of health policy as described in the health policy for Europe *(1)*.

Monitoring and evaluation of the attainment of the targets are important means of providing feedback to decision-makers. They can also help to involve the public, professionals, all relevant sectors and the mass media in the process of setting new targets, redefining old ones and creating initiatives for more effective policies. Thus, monitoring and evaluation not only give feedback on the implementation of a policy but also contribute to implementation and further development of the policy.

The technical implementation of monitoring involves many tasks and some problems. A national centre is needed to collect and analyse the data, to develop the collection system and to provide the available data to national and local governments, researchers and international organizations.

Obviously, international comparisons may give insight into the strengths and weaknesses of national alcohol policies, just as comparisons between regions and municipalities are important in developing local alcohol action. The trade in and advertising of alcohol are now an international business. Drinking patterns are being harmonized at the European level, and some alcohol problems are international, such as those related to tourism. Intergovernmental organizations, particularly the EU, have an increasing impact on national alcohol policies.

These factors show the growing need for target setting, monitoring and evaluation at the international level. Thus, all countries should have an interest in developing comparable data and an adequate database at the European level.

References

1. *Health for all targets. The health policy for Europe.* Copenhagen, WHO Regional Office for Europe, 1993 (European Health for All Series, No. 4).
2. MOSER, J. *Alcohol problems, policies and programmes in Europe.* Copenhagen, WHO Regional Office for Europe, 1992 (document EUR/ICP/ADA 011).
3. *European Alcohol Action Plan.* Copenhagen, WHO Regional Office for Europe, 1993 (document ICP/ADA 035).
4. *UK levels of health.* London, Faculty of Public Health Medicine of the Royal College of Physicians, 1991.
5. *Healthy people 2000. National health promotion and disease prevention objectives.* Washington, DC, US Government Printing Office, 1990.
6. GODFREY, C. & MAYNARD, A. *A health strategy for alcohol: setting targets and choosing policies.* York, Centre for Health Economics, 1992 (YARTIC Occasional Paper, No. 1).
7. MOSKALEWICZ, J. Alcohol as an economic issue: recent Polish experience. *Contemporary drug problems,* **18**(3): 407–415 (1991).
8. MÄKELA, K. *Unrecorded consumption of alcohol in Finland, 1950–1975.* Helsinki, Social Research Institute of Alcohol Studies, 1979 (Report No. 126).
9. OFFICE OF POPULATION CENSUSES AND SURVEYS. *General Household Survey.* London, H.M. Stationery Office, 1975–1992.
10. DEPARTMENT OF EMPLOYMENT. *Family Expenditure Survey.* London, H.M. Stationery Office, 1978–1992.
11. SIMPURA, J., ED. *Finnish drinking habits.* Helsinki, Finnish Foundation for Alcohol Studies, 1987, Vol 35.
12. KNIBBE, R. *Quantitative surveys on alcohol use.* Copenhagen, WHO Regional Office for Europe, 1992 (document).

13. GODDARD, E. *Drinking in England and Wales in the late 1980s*. London, H.M. Stationery Office, 1991.
14. HUPKENS, C. ET AL. Alcohol consumption in the European Community: uniformity and diversity in drinking patterns. *Addiction*, **88**(10): 1391–1404 (1993).
15. *Reader's Digest Eurodata – a consumer survey of 17 European countries*. New York, Reader's Digest Association, 1991.
16. WOLD, B., ED. *Health behaviour in school-aged children. A WHO cross-national survey (HBSC). Resource package of questions 1993–1994*. Bergen, Research Centre for Health Promotion, 1993.
17. *Alcohol and the public health. Report of the Faculty of Public Health Medicine of the Royal College of Physicians*. London, Macmillan Education, 1991.
18. *Alcohol, our favourite drug. Report of the Royal College of Psychiatrists*. London, Tavistock Publications, 1986.
19. *The medical consequences of alcohol abuse. Report of the Royal College of Physicians*. London, Tavistock Publications, 1987.
20. CENTERS FOR DISEASE CONTROL. Alcohol-related mortality and years of potential life lost – United States 1987. *Morbidity and mortality report*, **39**(11): 173–178 (1990).
21. *The quantification of drug-caused morbidity and mortality in Australia 1988. Part 1*. Canberra, Australian Government Publishing Service, 1990.
22. EDWARDS, G. ET AL. *Alcohol policy and the public good*. Oxford, Oxford University Press, 1994.
23. ANDERSON, P. ET AL. The risk of alcohol. *Addiction*, **88**(11): 1493–1508 (1993).
24. MARMOT, M. & BRUNNER, E. Alcohol and cardiovascular disease. *British medical journal*, **303**: 565–568 (1991).
25. WALD, I. & JAROSZEWSKI, Z. Alcohol consumption and alcohol psychoses in Poland. *Journal of studies on alcohol*, **44**(6): 1040–1048 (1983).
26. GODFREY, C. & HARDMAN, G. *Updating the social costs of alcohol misuse. Report to the Department of Health*. York, Centre for Health Economics, University of York, 1990.
27. ROMELSJÖ, A. The relationship between alcohol consumption and unintentional injury, violence, suicide and social complications. *In:* Edwards, G. & Holder, A., ED. *Alcohol policy – evidence and issues*. Oxford, Oxford University Press (in press).

28. MÄKELÄ, K. ET AL. *Alcohol, society and the state. Vol. 1. A comparative study of alcohol control.* Toronto, Addiction Research Foundation, 1981.
29. ÖSTERBERG, E. Would a more liberal control policy increase alcohol consumption? *Contemporary drug problems,* **17**: 545–573 (1990).
30. SKOG, O.-J. Future trends in alcohol consumption and alcohol related problems: anticipation in light of the efforts at harmonization in the European Community. *Contemporary drug problems,* **17**: 575–593 (1990).
31. LEHTO, J. *Approaches to alcohol control policy.* Copenhagen, WHO Regional Office for Europe, 1995 (WHO Regional Publications, European Series, No. 60).
32. SINGLE, E. The interaction between policy and research in the implementation of server training. *Addiction,* **88**(Suppl.): 105S–113S (1993).
33. BOOTH, M. ET AL. Industry: structure, performance and policy. *In*: Maynard, A. & Tether, P., ED. *Preventing alcohol and tobacco problems.* Aldershot, Avebury, 1990.
34. GIESBRECHT, N. ET AL., ED. *Research, action and the community: experiences in the prevention of alcohol and other drugs.* Washington, DC, US Government Printing Office, 1989.
35. PUSKA, P., ED. *Comprehensive cardiovascular community control programmes in Europe.* Copenhagen, WHO Regional Office for Europe, 1988 (EURO Reports and Studies, No. 106).
36. GIESBRECHT, N. *Community-based strategies to prevent the harm done by alcohol use.* Copenhagen, WHO Regional Office for Europe, 1992 (document).
37. PARTANEN, J. & MONTONEN, M. *Alcohol and the mass media.* Copenhagen, WHO Regional Office for Europe, 1988 (EURO Reports and Studies, No. 108).
38. ANDERSON, P. *Management of drinking problems.* Copenhagen, WHO Regional Office for Europe, 1990 (WHO Regional Publications, European Series, No. 32).
39. RICHMOND, R. & ANDERSON, P. Research in general practice for smokers and excessive drinkers: the experience in Australia and the UK. III. Dissemination of interventions. *Addiction,* **89**(1): 49–62 (1994).

40. INSTITUTE OF MEDICINE. *Broadening the base of treatment for alcohol problems*. Washington, DC, National Academy Press, 1990.
41. RUSH, B. A systems approach to estimating the required capacity of alcohol treatment services. *British journal of addiction*, **85**: 49–59 (1990).
42. PRODUKTSCHAP VOOR GEDISTILLEERDE DRANKEN. *World drink trends 1993*. Henley-on-Thames, NTC Publications, 1993.
43. ÖSTERBERG, E. Recorded and unrecorded alcohol consumption. *In*: Simpura, J., ED. *Finnish drinking habits*. Helsinki, Finnish Foundation for Alcohol Studies, 1987, Vol 35.
44. POPHAM, R.E. Indirect methods of alcoholism prevalence estimation. A critical evaluation. *In*: Popham, R.E., ED. *Alcohol and alcoholism*. Toronto, University of Toronto Press, 1970, pp. 678–685.
45. MANN, R.E. ET AL. Are decreases in liver cirrhosis rates a result of increased treatment for alcoholism? *British journal of addiction*, **83**: 683–688 (1988).
46. *Alcohol and accidents*. London, British Medical Association, 1989.
47. CASSELMAN, J. & MOORTHAMER, L. *Violent social behaviour and alcohol use*. Copenhagen, WHO Regional Office for Europe, 1988 (document EUR/ICP/ADA 014).
48. DUNBAR, J. Drinking and driving what can we learn from other countries? *In*: *Alcohol and traffic in Europe*. Brussels, International Abstaining Motorists' Association, 1992.
49. *The ICD-10 classification of mental and behavioural disorders*. Geneva, World Health Organization, 1992.
50. SKOG, O.-J. The prevention of alcoholism and drinking problems – who are the target groups? *In*: Aasland, O.G., ED. *The negative social consequences of alcohol use*. Oslo, Norwegian Ministry of Health and Social Affairs, 1991.
51. *AUDIT. The alcohol use disorders identification test: guidelines for use in primary health care*. Geneva, World Health Organization, 1989 (document WHO/PSA/92.4).
52. *The health of the nation. A strategy for health in England*. London, H.M. Stationery Office, 1992.
53. DAVIES, P. & WALSH, D. *Alcohol problems and alcohol control in Europe*. London, Croom Helm, 1983.

54. CONTEL, M. L'approccio istituzionale e normativo [Institutional and normative approach]. *In*: *Alcool: consumi e politiche* [Alcohol: consumption and policy]. Rome, Permanent Observatory on Youth and Alcohol, 1993.
55. KLINGEMANN, H. ET AL. *European summary on drug abuse*. Copenhagen, WHO Regional Office for Europe, 1992 (document EUR/ICP/ADA 527/A).
56. *Tobacco alert*. Geneva, World Health Organization, July 1993 (newsletter).
57. *Handlingsprogram för att minska alkoholkonsumtionen med minst 25 procent till är 2000. Del 1. Förebyggande insatser.* [Action programme to reduce alcohol consumption by at least 25% by the year 2000. Part 1. Preventive efforts]. Stockholm, National Board of Health and Welfare, 1990.
58. *Trends in alcohol and drug use in Sweden*. Stockholm, Swedish Council for Information on Alcohol and Other Drugs, 1991 (Report Series, No. 17).
59. HAUT COMITÉ D'ÉTUDE ET D'INFORMATION SUR L'ALCOOLISME. *La mortalité 1991*. Paris, Documentation Française, 1991.
60. *Alcohol and drugs in Norway*. Oslo, National Directorate for the Prevention of Alcohol and Drug Problems, 1993.
61. *Alkohol- og narkotikamisbruget 1990–1991* [Alcohol and drug misuse 1990–1991]. Copenhagen, National Board of Health, 1992.
62. *Zahlen und Fakten zu Alkohol und anderen Drogen 1993*. Lausanne, SFA/ISPA, 1993.
63. *Health plan for Catalonia 1993–1995*. Barcelona, Department of Health and Social Security, 1993.
64. RITSON, B. *Community and municipal action on alcohol*. Copenhagen, WHO Regional Office for Europe, 1995 (WHO Regional Publications, European Series, No. 63).
65. *The role of general practice settings in the prevention and management of the harm done by alcohol use*: report on a WHO meeting. Copenhagen, WHO Regional Office for Europe, 1992 (document EUR/ICP/ADA 038).
66. *A multi-city action plan on alcohol*: report on a WHO preparatory meeting. Copenhagen, WHO Regional Office for Europe, 1993 (document EUR/ICP/ADA 039B).

67. *Proposal for a Healthy City Plan of the City of Copenhagen 1994–1997*. Copenhagen, Copenhagen Health Services, 1994.
68. *Twenty steps for developing a Healthy Cities project*. Copenhagen, WHO Regional Office for Europe, 1992 (document ICP/HSC 644).
69. THORSEN, T. & SOLGAARD, D. *Alcohol profile of the city of Copenhagen*. Copenhagen, City of Copenhagen, 1993.
70. OXFORD CITY COUNCIL. *A balanced alcohol strategy for Oxford*. Oxford, City of Oxford, 1990.

Annex 1

Targets for Health for All

Target 1 – Equity in Health

By the year 2000, the differences in health status between countries and between groups within countries should be reduced by at least 25%, by improving the level of health of disadvantaged nations and groups.

Target 2 – Health and Quality of Life

By the year 2000, all people should have the opportunity to develop and use their own health potential in order to lead socially, economically and mentally fulfilling lives.

Target 3 – Better Opportunities for People with Disabilities

By the year 2000, people with disabilities should be able to lead socially, economically and mentally fulfilling lives with the support of special arrangements that improve their relative physical, social and economic opportunities.

Target 4 – Reducing Chronic Disease

By the year 2000, there should be a sustained and continuing reduction in morbidity and disability due to chronic disease in the Region.

Target 5 – Reducing Communicable Disease

By the year 2000, there should be no indigenous cases of poliomyelitis, diphtheria, neonatal tetanus, measles, mumps and congenital rubella in the Region and there should be a sustained and continuing reduction in the incidence and adverse consequences of other communicable diseases, notably HIV infection.

Target 6 – Healthy Aging

By the year 2000, life expectancy at birth in the Region should be at least 75 years and there should be a sustained and continuing improvement in the health of all people aged 65 years and over.

Target 7 – Health of Children and Young People

By the year 2000, the health of all children and young people should be improved, giving them the opportunity to grow and develop to their full physical, mental and social potential.

Target 8 – Health of Women

By the year 2000, there should be sustained and continuing improvement in the health of all women.

Target 9 – Reducing Cardiovascular Disease

By the year 2000, mortality from diseases of the circulatory system should be reduced, in the case of people under 65 years by at least 15%, and there should be progress in improving the quality of life of all people suffering from cardiovascular disease.

Target 10 – Controlling Cancer

By the year 2000, mortality from cancer in people under 65 years should be reduced by at least 15% and the quality of life of all people with cancer should be significantly improved.

Target 11 – Accidents

By the year 2000, injury, disability and death arising from accidents should be reduced by at least 25%.

Target 12 – Reducing Mental Disorders and Suicide

By the year 2000, there should be a sustained and continuing reduction in the prevalence of mental disorders, an improvement in the quality of life of all people with such disorders, and a reversal of the rising trends in suicide and attempted suicide.

Target 13 – Healthy Public Policy

By the year 2000, all Member States should have developed, and be implementing, intersectoral policies for the promotion of healthy lifestyles, with systems ensuring public participation in policy-making and implementation.

Target 14 – Settings for Health Promotion

By the year 2000, all settings of social life and activity, such as the city, school, workplace, neighbourhood and home, should provide greater opportunities for promoting health.

Target 15 – Health Competence

By the year 2000, accessible and effective education and training in health promotion should be available in all Member States, in order to improve public and professional competence in promoting health and increasing health awareness in other sectors.

Target 16 – Healthy Living

By the year 2000, there should be continuous efforts in all Member States to actively promote and support healthy patterns of living through balanced nutrition, appropriate physical activity, healthy sexuality, good stress management and other aspects of positive health behaviour.

Target 17 – Tobacco, Alcohol and Psychoactive Drugs

By the year 2000, the health-damaging consumption of dependence-producing substances such as alcohol, tobacco and psychoactive drugs should have been significantly reduced in all Member States.

Target 18 – Policy on Environment and Health

By the year 2000, all Member States should have developed, and be implementing, policies on the environment and health that ensure ecologically sustainable development, effective prevention and control of environmental health risks and equitable access to healthy environments.

Target 19 – Environmental Health Management

By the year 2000, there should be effective management systems and resources in all Member States for putting policies on environment and health into practice.

Target 20 – Water Quality

By the year 2000, all people should have access to adequate supplies of safe drinking-water, and the pollution of groundwater sources, rivers, lakes and seas should no longer pose a threat to health.

Target 21 – Air Quality

By the year 2000, air quality in all countries should be improved to a point at which recognized air pollutants do not pose a threat to public health.

Target 22 – Food Quality and Safety

By the year 2000, health risks due to microorganisms or their toxins, to chemicals and to radioactivity in food should have been significantly reduced in all Member States.

Target 23 – Waste Management and Soil Pollution

By the year 2000, public health risks caused by solid and hazardous wastes and soil pollution should be effectively controlled in all Member States.

Target 24 – Human Ecology and Settlements

By the year 2000, cities, towns and rural communities throughout the Region should offer physical and social environments supportive to the health of their inhabitants.

Target 25 – Health of People at Work

By the year 2000, the health of workers in all Member States should be improved by making work environments more healthy, reducing work-related disease and injury, and promoting the wellbeing of people at work.

Target 26 – Health Service Policy

By the year 2000, all Member States should have developed, and be implementing, policies that ensure universal access to health services of quality, based on primary care and supported by secondary and tertiary care.

Target 27 – Health Service Resources and Management

By the year 2000, health service systems in all Member States should be managed cost-effectively, with resources being distributed according to need.

Target 28 – Primary Health Care

By the year 2000, primary health care in all Member States should meet the basic health needs of the population by providing a wide range of health-promotive, curative, rehabilitative and supportive services and by actively supporting self-help activities of individuals, families and groups.

Target 29 – Hospital Care

By the year 2000, hospitals in all Member States should be providing cost-effective secondary and tertiary care and contribute actively to improving health status and patient satisfaction.

Target 30 – Community Services to Meet Special Needs

By the year 2000, people in all Member States needing long-term care and support should have access to appropriate services of a high quality.

Target 31 – Quality of Care and Appropriate Technology

By the year 2000, there should be structures and processes in all Member States to ensure continuous improvement in the quality of health care and appropriate development and use of health technologies.

Target 32 – Health Research and Development

By the year 2000, health research should strengthen the acquisition and application of knowledge in support of health for all development in all Member States.

Target 33 – Health for All Policy Development

By the year 2000, all Member States should have developed, and be implementing, policies in line with the concepts and principles of the European health for all policy, balancing lifestyle, environment and health service concerns.

Target 34 – Managing Health for All Development

By the year 2000, management structures and processes should exist in all Member States to inspire, guide and coordinate health development, in line with health for all principles.

Target 35 – Health Information Support

By the year 2000, health information systems in all Member States should actively support the formulation, implementation, monitoring and evaluation of health for all policies.

Target 36 – Developing Human Resources for Health

By the year 2000, education and training of health and other personnel in all Member States should actively contribute to the achievement of health for all.

Target 37 – Partners for Health

By the year 2000, in all Member States, a wide range of organizations and groups throughout the public, private and voluntary sectors should be actively contributing to the achievement of health for all.

Target 38 – Health and Ethics

By the year 2000, all Member States should have mechanisms in place to strengthen ethical considerations in decisions relating to the health of individuals, groups and populations.

Annex 2

Alcohol Consumption Surveys

Surveys of rather small, representative samples of the population can give valuable information about the distribution of alcohol consumption in general and high-risk consumption in particular. When surveys are repeated with the same methodology and within reasonable intervals, they can be used to monitor changes in alcohol consumption patterns.

Surveys other than those of drinking habits may include questions on alcohol consumption. The information provided by one study can be compared with that from others if they use the same methodology to ask about alcohol use. Everybody would benefit from the use of standard questions and methodology.

International standardization of survey questions and methodology may be more difficult, because questions might have different meanings in different drinking cultures. Nevertheless, the use of some questions and similar methodology would assist international comparisons.

THE SAMPLE

The sufficiency of the size of the sample depends on the specificity of analysis that is planned. For example, if heavy drinkers are to be studied by sex, age and socioeconomic group, a general population sample should be large enough to include sufficient numbers of heavy drinkers in each subgroup. National surveys, with 1500–4000 respondents, have achieved rather good results *(1,2)*.

Defects in the sample framework might produce bias in the results, if population groups with particular drinking patterns are excluded from the sample or if their response rate is significantly lower than the average. Many surveys exclude from the sample people who are homeless or living in an institution or in university or other temporary residences. In addition, some studies indicate that heavy drinkers are more difficult to contact and are thus more frequently categorized as non-respondents than older married people with lower consumption *(3)*. Other studies, however, have found that abstainers might comprise a disproportionately large share of the non-respondents, and that the response rate of heavy drinkers is at the average level *(1)*.

UNDERREPORTING OF DRINKING

Most people tend to underreport the amounts of alcoholic beverages that they have drunk. There are many reasons for this *(1–3)*. For example, it is difficult to remember exactly what one has drunk in the last week or two. This is also true for non-alcoholic beverages and many other aspects of consumption. In addition, it is difficult to estimate exactly the amounts that one has drunk, especially the drinks taken at home or served by friends.

Further, people may underreport drinking that contravenes the social norms for normal consumption, such as drinking in the morning, during working hours, before driving a car or in excessive amounts. Finally, the dates of the survey may lead to the reporting of too small a share of annual consumption if there is a great seasonal variation in drinking and the survey is made when consumption is low.

In many countries, the total alcohol consumption estimated directly from survey data comprises around 35–60% of the total consumption measured by the official sales records *(1)*. The proportion of underreporting is often supposed not to vary much between different population groups and drinking levels. While this has not been studied thoroughly, there are no indications of great variation between population groups in this respect *(1,2)*.

ASKING ABOUT ALCOHOL CONSUMPTION

In some studies, such as the international survey on the health behaviour of school-age children, the objective is not to estimate the total individual consumption but to obtain information on the starting age of drinking and frequency of drinking and intoxication *(4)*. Thus, the survey can use rather simple questions (Table 1).

When the objective is to estimate the total individual consumption, more detailed questions are needed to minimize the problems of underreporting or occasional overreporting. Three different methodologies are most often used to measure individual consumption *(1–3,5)*:

- a diary estimate, in which the respondents record their daily alcohol use in a diary once a day for one to several weeks;
- a retrospective diary estimate, in which the respondents are asked to recall their alcohol use during all drinking occasions on each day to be investigated, with the period covered including the previous seven days, at least one week or, for those who drink more infrequently, a longer period chosen to contain roughly four occasions of consumption; and
- a usual consumption estimate, in which the respondents are asked to classify their drinking habits in terms of usual frequency of drinking occasions and the usual quantity of different alcoholic beverages drunk on these occasions.

The diary estimate seems to result in the best coverage of actual consumption, followed by the retrospective diary estimate. The usual consumption estimate is also often used, although it seems to result in lower coverage.

The exact questions used in these methodologies may need to vary from country to country, to reflect the different drinking cultures. Tables 1–3 present three sets of questions *(2,4,6)*. The Finnish survey includes not only questions about consumption but also a retrospective diary.

ESTIMATING THE ALCOHOL CONSUMPTION OF RESPONDENTS

Normally, the answers to survey questions cannot be directly used as estimates of the annual consumption of the respondent. A number of adjustments are needed:

- the multiplication of the consumption in the period studied by the number of such periods in a year;
- an adjustment for seasonal variation if necessary; and
- an adjustment for the underreporting of consumption.

REFERENCES

1. KNIBBE, R. *Quantitative surveys on alcohol use.* Copenhagen, WHO Regional Office for Europe, 1992 (document).
2. SIMPURA, J., ED. *Finnish drinking habits.* Helsinki, Finnish Foundation for Alcohol Studies, 1987, Vol. 35.
3. DUFFY J. *Quantitative surveys on alcohol use. Routinely collected national data.* Copenhagen, WHO Regional Office for Europe, 1992 (document).
4. WOLD, B., ED. *Health behaviour in school-aged children. A WHO cross-national survey (HBSC). Resource package of questions 1993–1994.* Bergen, Research Centre for Health Promotion, 1993.
5. GODDARD, E. *Drinking in England and Wales in the late 1980s.* London, H.M. Stationery Office, 1991.
6. DE BRUIN, A. ET AL., ED. *Common instruments in health interview surveys.* Copenhagen, WHO Regional Office for Europe (in press).

Table 1. The questions of a study on the drinking of school-age children

1. Did you ever drink one of the following beverages? (at least a whole glass, not just tasting)

	Yes	No
Beer		
Wine		
Cider		
Liquor		

2. At present, how often do you drink anything alcoholic, such as wine, liquor or beer? Try to include even those times when you only drink a small amount.

	Every day	Every week	Every month	Less than once a month	Never
Beer					
Wine					
Liquor					
Cider					

3. If at present you drink an alcoholic beverage at least once every week, how old were you when you began to do so?

   I was about _______ years old.

4. Have you ever had so much alcohol that you really were drunk?

   No, never.
   Yes, once.
   Yes, 2–3 times.
   Yes, 4–10 times.
   Yes, more than 10 times.

5. If you have ever been drunk, how old were you when you were drunk for the first time?

   I was about _______ years old.

Source: Wold *(4)*.

Table 2. Sample sets of questions on alcohol consumption

A. Questions to produce estimates on the number of drinkers and very rough estimates of frequency of drinking and amount of drinking

A1. How long ago did you last have an alcoholic drink?

(a) During the last week
(b) One week to 1 month ago
(c) One month to 3 months ago — Go to A2
(d) Three months to 12 months ago
(e) More than 12 months ago — End

A2. During the past [week, 2 weeks, etc.] on how many days did you drink alcohol, such as [list culturally specific illustrations]?

Number of days _______

A3. On the days that you drank alcohol, how many [drinks, glasses, etc.] did you have, on average?

Number of [drinks, glasses, etc.] _______

A4. Was your drinking in the past two weeks typical of your usual drinking in the past year?

Yes ___ End
No ___ Go to A5

A5. Was your drinking in the past two weeks more or less than your drinking in the past year?

More ___
Less ___

B. Questions that can be used for same purpose as in A, if the survey is conducted in a short calendar period and it is a period of typical drinking patterns in the study population

B1. How long ago did you last have an alcoholic drink?

(a) During the last week
(b) One week to 1 month ago
(c) One month to 3 months ago — Go to B2
(d) Three months to 12 months ago
(e) More than 12 months ago — End

Table 2 (contd)

B2. Thinking about your drinking in the last year, did you usually drink alcohol, such as [list culturally specific illustrations] on some days of the week?

Yes ____ Go to B3
No ____ End

B3. On how many days during the week did you usually drink alcohol, on average?

Number of days ____

B4. On the days that you drank alcohol, how many [drinks, glasses, etc.] did you have, on average?

Number of [drinks, glasses, etc.] ____

C. Questions to obtain a somewhat more accurate estimate on the frequency and amounts drunk and to classify respondents into types of drinkers (low- and high-risk drinkers)

C1. Please indicate on the following list which alcoholic beverages you drank in the last 12 months, even if only once.

____ Beer
____ Wine, sherry, port, vermouth
____ Liqueur, advocaat
____ Gin, brandy, cognac, whisky, vodka
____ Long drinks
____ Low-alcohol beverages
____ I have not drunk any alcohol in the last twelve months

C2. During the last six months, have you ever had six or more drinks containing alcohol in one day?

Yes ____ Go to C3
No ____ Go to C4

Table 2 (contd)

C3. During the last six months, how often have you had six or more drinks containing alcohol in one day?

____ Every day
____ 5–6 times a week
____ 3–4 times a week
____ 1–2 times a week
____ 1–3 times a month
____ 3–5 times in six months
____ 1–2 times in six months

C4. Do you usually drink alcohol on weekdays (Monday–Thursday)?

Yes ____
No ____

C5. On how many of the four weekdays do you usually drink alcohol?

____ 1 day
____ 2 days
____ 3 days
____ 4 days

C6. How many glasses on average do you drink on such a day?

____ 11 or more glasses, namely ___ glasses
____ 7–10 glasses
____ 6 glasses
____ 4–5 glasses
____ 3 glasses
____ 2 glasses
____ 1 glass

C7. Do you usually drink alcohol on the weekend (Friday–Sunday)?

Yes____
No ____

Table 2 (contd)

C8. On how many of the three weekend days do you usually drink alcohol?

____ 1 day
____ 2 days
____ 3 days

C9. How many glasses on average do you drink on such a day?

____ 11 or more glasses, namely ____ glasses
____ 7–10 glasses
____ 6 glasses
____ 4–5 glasses
____ 3 glasses
____ 2 glasses
____ 1 glass

Source: De Bruin et al. *(6)*.

Table 3. The alcchol consumption questions of a Finnish survey of drinking habits

1. How often do you drink alcoholic beverages?

	Daily	4–5 times weekly	A couple of times per week	Once a week	A couple of times per month	About once a month	About once every couple of months	3–4 times a year	Once or twice a year	Less than once a year	Never
Beer	1	2	3	4	5	6	7	8	9	10	11
Wine	1	2	3	4	5	6	7	8	9	10	11
Spirits	1	2	3	4	5	6	7	8	9	10	11

2. And when you drink, about how much do you consume at a time? Please respond using the alternatives listed.

2.1 Beer		2.2. Wine		2.3 Spirits	
Less than a bottle	1	Half a glass	1	One shot (about 4 cl)	1
1 bottle	2	A glassful	2	A couple of shots (about 7–8 cl)	2
1–2 bottles (about ½ litre)	3	A couple of glasses	3	About 3 shots (about 1 dl)	3
2 bottles	4	Slightly less than a half bottle	4	About 4 shots	4
3 bottles (about 1 litre)	5	About 1 half bottle	5	5–6 shots	5
4–5 bottles	6	Slightly less than a bottle	6	A little less than a half bottle (about 3 dl)	6
6–9 bottles (2–3 litres)	7	About 1 bottle	7	About 1 half bottle	7
10 bottles or more	8	More than 1 bottle	8	One half-litre bottle or more	8
I have never drunk beer or I have only just tasted it	9	I have never drunk wine or I have only just tasted it	9	I have never drunk spirits or I have only just tasted it	9

Table 3 (contd)

		Daily	4–5 times weekly	A couple of times per week	Once a week	A couple of times per month	About once a month	About once every couple of months	3–4 times a year	Once or twice a year	Less than once a year	Never
3.	How often do you visit a restaurant with the intent to drink?	1	2	3	4	5	6	7	8	9	10	11
4.	How often do you visit cafés licensed to sell mild beer to consume this kind of beer?	1	2	3	4	5	6	7	8	9	10	11
5.	How often do you use alcohol altogether?[a]	1	2	3	4	5	6	7	8	9	10	11
	[a] *In your assessment try to include also those occasions when you have consumed insignificant amounts of alcohol, even just half a bottle of mild beer or a sip of wine.*											
6.	How often do you drink enough to feel it a little?	1	2	3	4	5	6	7	8	9	10	11
7.	How often do you drink enough really to feel it?	1	2	3	4	5	6	7	8	9	10	11

Table 3 (contd)

Next the respondent is asked to record in detail the most recent drinking occasions, even those where only a sip of alcohol was consumed. The period from which the drinking occasions are recorded depends on the drinking frequency of the respondent (question 5 above) according to the following formula.

	Drinking frequency	Recording period
1.	Daily	One week
2.	4–5 times a week	One week
3.	A couple of times a week	Two weeks
4.	Once a week	Four weeks
5.	A couple of times a month	Two months
6.	About once a month	Four months
7.	About once every two months	Eight months
8.	3–4 times a year	Twelve months
9.	Once or twice a year	Twelve months
10.	Less than once a year	Twelve months

Regarding each drinking occasion a couple of questions are asked (date, character of the occasion, location, etc.). Then the respondent is asked to answer the following question separately for each drinking occasion.

8. What beverage did you yourself drink and how much? Record amount by beverage type.

Mild beer	___ bottles	___ cans	Fortified wines	___ cl
Strong beer	___ bottles	___ cans	Spirits	___ cl
Premixed drinks	___ bottles		Pharmaceutical alcohol	___ cl
Home-brewed beer	___ cl		Moonshine	___ cl
Kilju (a Finnish home brew)	___ cl		Home-made wine	___ cl
Wines	___ cl		Non-beverage alcohol (drops, cough medicines, etc.)	___ cl

Source: Simpura (*2*).